How to Play Chess

A Beginner's Guide to Learning the Chess Game, Pieces, Board, Rules & Strategies

Table of Contents

Chapter 1: Introduction 1

Chapter 2: How to play..5

Chapter 3: Basic Strategies 39

Chapter 4: Beginner strategies 45

Chapter 5: Chess: the players and the changes 55

Chapter 6: Checkmate: the conclusion...59

What is chess?

Chess is a two-player board game, played on a board of 64 squares. The chessboard is an eight-by-eight grid of alternating black and white squares (sometimes the colors can differ, but black and white are the most common colors). Each player has sixteen pieces which can move in a variety of ways (this will be explained later). The pieces are also either black or white; a white set for one player and a black set for the other player (again colors can vary). You can capture opponent pieces by landing on the same square as that piece and the object of the game is to put the opponent's king in such a position that they cannot make a move without their king being captured. When this happens it is deemed 'checkmate' and the game is over. A simple game which takes minutes to learn and a lifetime to master.

Chapter 1
Introduction

History

Chess really is the game of Kings! A game of intellectuals and commoners, the rich and the poor, the revered and the forgotten, the human race. Who you are outside of the board does not matter, for on the board you can be king.

The *Shahnameh* is an epic poem by the Persian poet Ferdowsi in which he offers an apocryphal account of the origins of the game of chess. Talhand and Gav are two half-brothers who are in competition for the throne of India. After meeting in battle, Talhand dies on his elephant without a wound. Their mother is distraught, she believes that Gav has killed his half-brother and when Gav tries to explain what happens, she does not believe him. The wise men of the day invent the game of chess to depict the events of the battle, through this they able to show the mother of the princes that Talhad, surrounded by all of his enemies, died of fatigue. The poem uses the term 'Shah Mat' (checkmate) to describe Talhand's fate.

I love to imagine this alternate origin of the game of chess, but it is hard to argue with the historians who have traced the early beginnings of chess back to the Kushan Empire in ancient Afghanistan, dating this around 50BC-200AD. The precursor to chess brings us to the 6th century and the game we now know as chess originated somewhere around the 15th century in Europe.

The game of chaturanga was played in India during the Gupta Empire as early as the 6th century. chaturanga translates as 'four divisions' and describes the four divisions of the military; infantry, cavalry, elephantry, and chariotry. These four divisions became the modern day pawn (infantry), knight (cavalry), bishop (elephantry) and rook (chariotry). I do not like to ponder the transformation from elephant to bishop.

From India, the game was taken to Persia and became part of the education of nobilities. Around the year 600AD, the name was shortened to chatrang, then evolved to shatranj; the Arab's lack of *ch* and *ng* sounds contributing to this. During this time the rules began to evolve. The word 'Shah' is Perian for 'King', and when attaching the opposing king; 'Shah Mat' translated to 'The king is helpless'. If you have a basic knowledge of chess terminology then you can predict the evolution of 'Shah' to 'check' and "Shah Mat' to 'Checkmate' (we will discuss these terms late in the book).

After the Islamic conquest of Persia, the game was enjoyed throughout the Muslim world. The pieces kept their Persian names, but as the game spread across Europe the name began to change once more. Some countries, such as Spain and Greece, derived their name for chess from the name 'shatranj', becoming 'acedrex' or 'zatrikion'. While other countries derived new names from the word for king. In Dutch the game was now 'schaken' and in Italian, it was 'scacchi'.

Introduction

Chess spread to Western Europe by many routes and then across the world. By the 15th century, chess had almost taken the shape of the modern game. As we travel to the modern day we see important additions such as reference books, tournaments, variations, timers, rules and most importantly; the players.

Fast forward to the 1880s and we are in the midst of the 'Romantic Era of Chess'. I dare you to find another game which has had the fortune of finding an era of romance. This romantic era was a characterization of the swashbuckling attacks a pirate may spring, the clever combinations of the wisest heroes of our folklore, the brash sacrifices our ancestors may have played out in their own lives and the dynamic games we all play in our minds. The focus was more on the artistic expression of your game and how you won, rather than the technical aspects, future planning or winning itself.

The romantic era was followed by a more scientific one. In the second half of the 19th, modern chess tournaments began, the first world tournament being held in 1886. From 1945, the Russians become dominant in the game of chess until Bobby Fisher, from the USA, became the champion in the mid-1970s. In 1999, current champion Gary Kasparov played an online game against 50,000 people from 75 countries in what was to be one of the most important chess games in theory and research. After 62 games and four months, Kasparov won.

Chapter 2
How to play

The board

The board is an eight-by-eight grid of alternating black and white squares. Sixty-four squares in total. Take your board and look at it, turn it in your hands, visualize the game you are about to play. Smell the wood of the board (or plastic, metal perhaps, maybe hold back if you are playing on a computer screen). If you have an opponent, place the board so that it is sitting between the two of you and make sure that there is a white square at the bottom right-hand corner, this is the correct set-up for your chess board. Your board is in place, now let us look at the pieces.

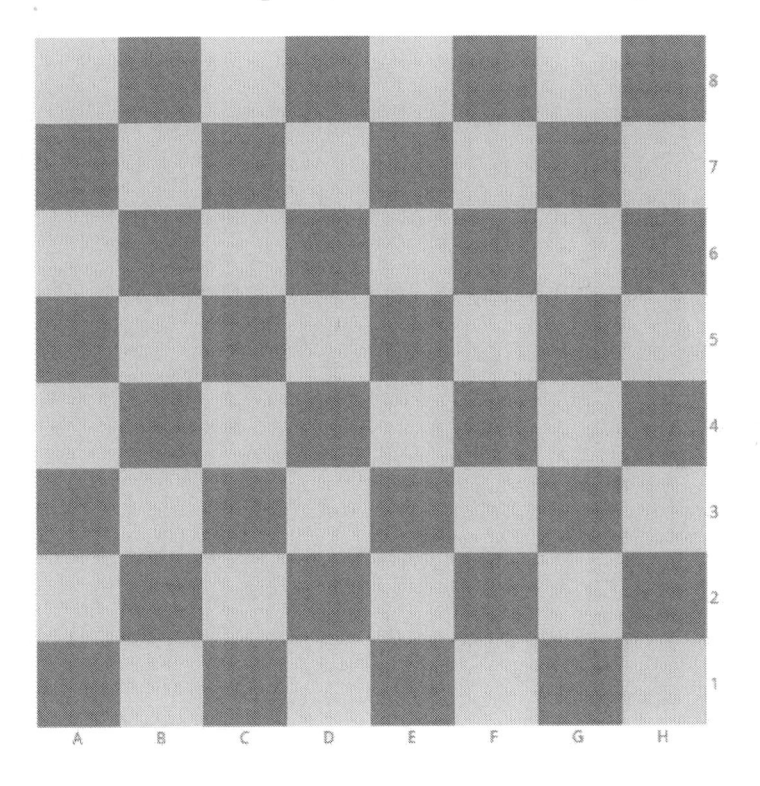

The pieces

Each player should have sixteen pieces in total; one player will have white pieces and one will have black (sometimes the colors are different, but as long as you have two different colors then we are ready to play). Amongst the sixteen pieces, there are six different characters.

Eight of the pieces will be pawns, these are typically shorter pieces with a spherical head. While they are often the most sacrifice pieces of the game, they are still very important to you winning.

Two pieces are rooks and look like the turrets of castles.

Two pieces are knights and will often look like horses.

Two pieces are bishops and will appear to be wearing bishop hats.

One piece is the queen, who will often display a rounded crown, she is the most powerful piece in the game. The last piece is the king, who will be wearing a pointed crown, he is the most important player in the game. While his motion is limited, if you fail to defend him properly, then you will quickly lose.

Queens:

Kings:

Set-up

Familiarize yourself with the pieces and we will set up the board. The chessboard will be set-up the same way for each and every game. Your sixteen pieces will fill your two closest rows of your board. Imagine the board is a theater and each square is a seat. From left to right we have the rows.

The second row is filled with your eight pawns, they are your first line of defense. Go ahead and place your pawns.

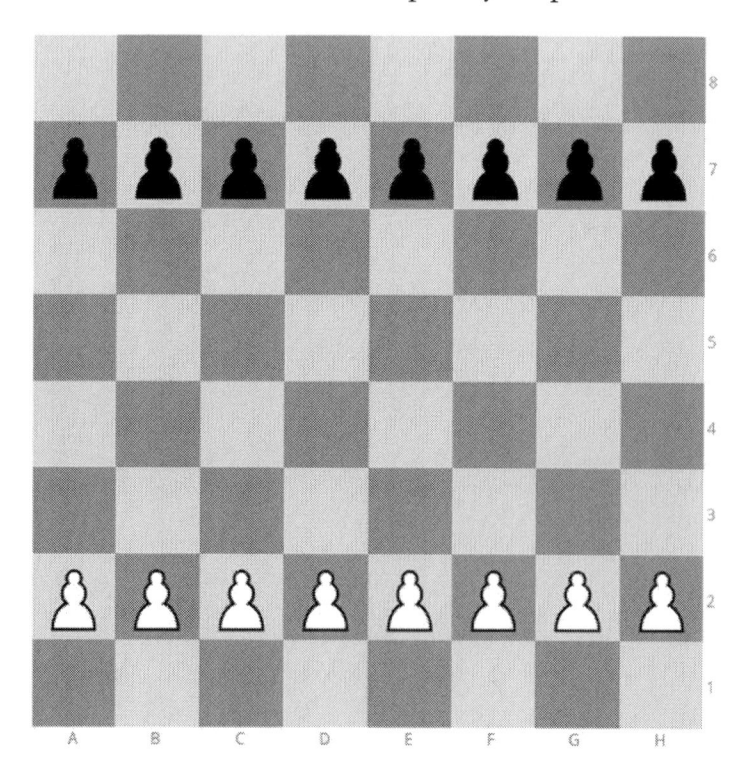

How to play

Now we will fill our first row (the row closest to us). At each corner place a rook.

Next to each rook place a knight.

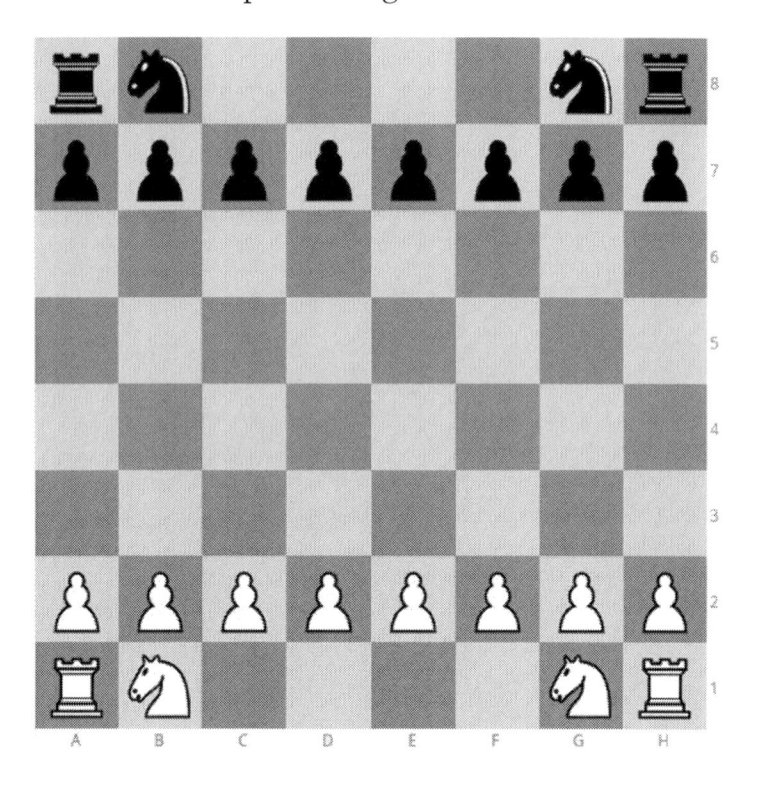

How to play

Next to each knight place a bishop.

We now have two squares left. The queen always goes on her matching color. So if you are white, then the queen will go on the remaining white square. If you are playing as black, then the queen will go on the remaining black square. Once you have placed your queen, the king will find its home on the one remaining square. Now that we are set up, we are almost ready to begin.

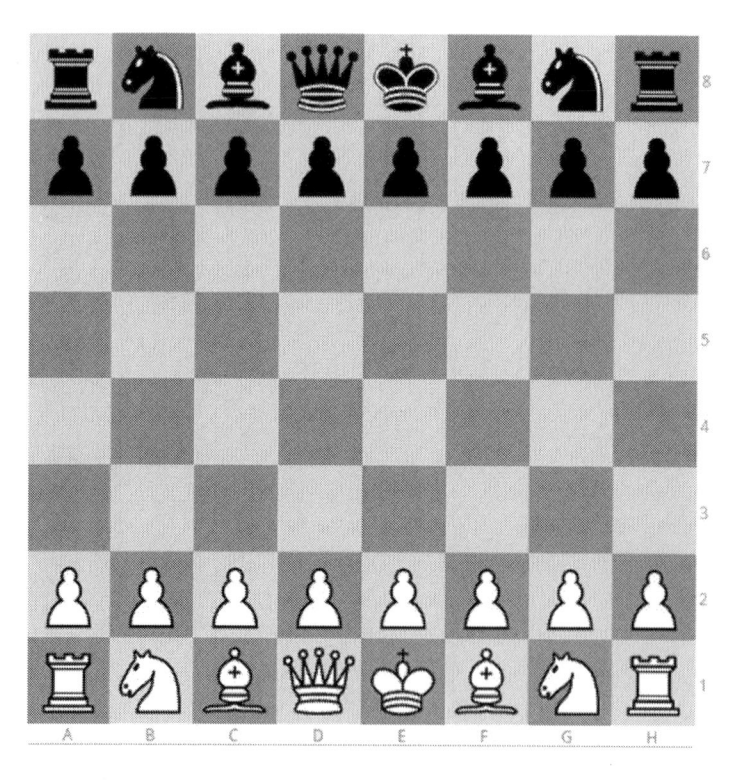

Moves

This is one of the hardest parts for beginners; memorizing all of the moves. Not only do you need to know where your pieces can move, but you should also be watching for where your opponent's pieces can move. This is where chess begins to become more complicated, but for now, we will focus only on how each of the pieces can move.

Typically pieces can only move to squares where there is no obstructions in-between, pieces cannot jump over other pieces. There is one exception to this which will be detailed below. Pieces cannot land on a square which contains a piece of the same color. When a piece lands on a square which has a piece of the opposite color then we say that that piece has been 'captured' and it is removed from the board. Capturing a piece ends a turn.

The **pawn** makes up half of your pieces, but as a piece, is one of the most limited in movement, often becoming trapped on the board or used to stop the oncoming opponent pawns.

Pawns can only *move* forward. They can move forward one space at a time, except on their first move where they can move two. They cannot move backward, side-to-side or diagonally. This means that when they are on the second row, they have not yet moved. When they are on the second row you have the option of moving the pawn forward one space or two. Once a pawn is no longer on the second row the move must have taken place previous. This means that the pawn can only move one space from now on. Simple right?

How to Play Chess

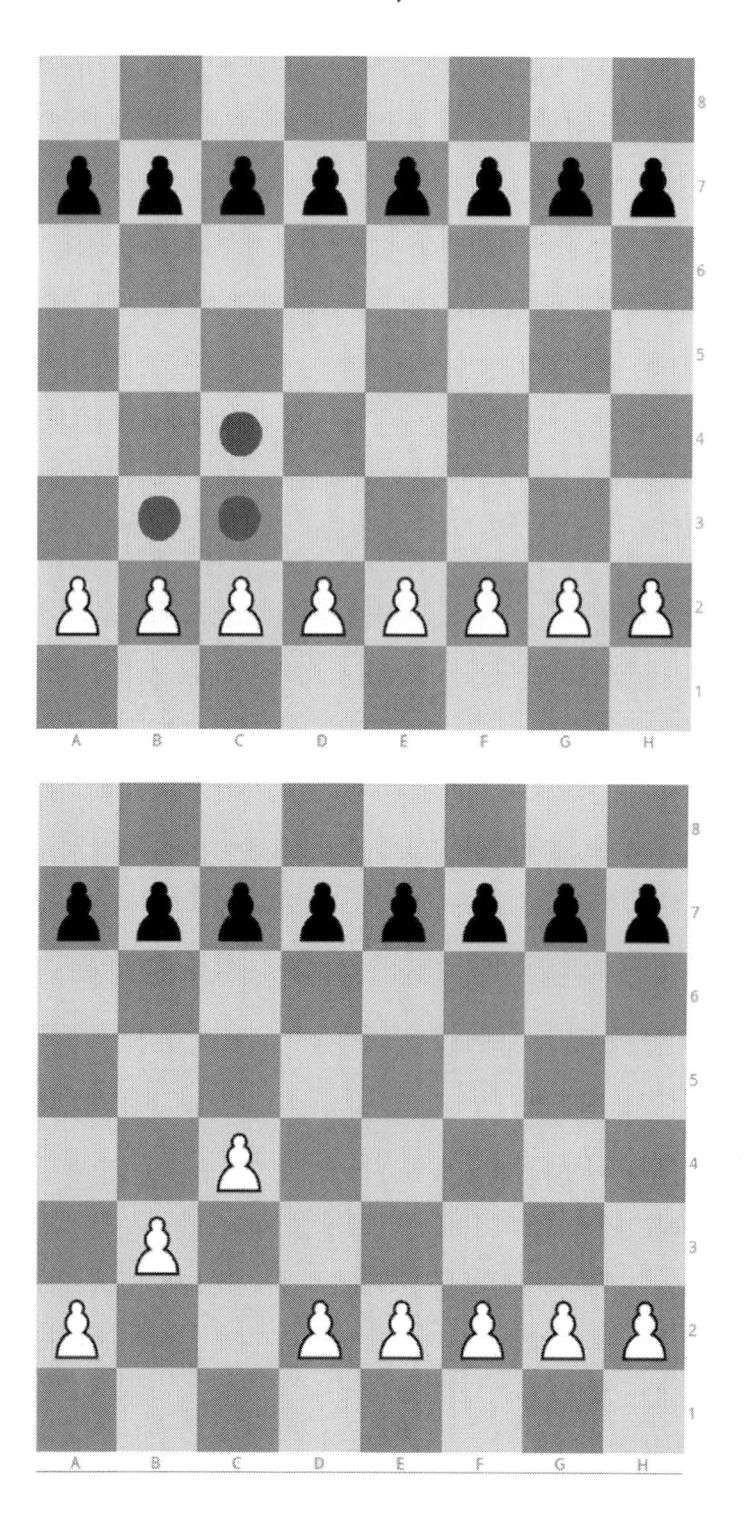

14

Sounded simple, but I am about to spring this:

Pawns can only *capture* diagonally. Confusing right? While pawns can only move forward, they can only capture an opponent piece diagonally. And since they can only move forward, then it makes sense that they can only capture another piece diagonally in front of them. Imagine pawns as progress, progress always marches forward.

The **rook** can move up, down, left or right. The rook can move as many spaces in the given direction that it wants, as long as it is not blocked by another piece. For example, if the rook wanted to move right across the board and there is nothing blocking it, then you could choose to move the rook one space, three spaces or even seven spaces. The flexibility to move this piece so quickly across the board makes this an interesting character in the game of chess, especially in the end game.

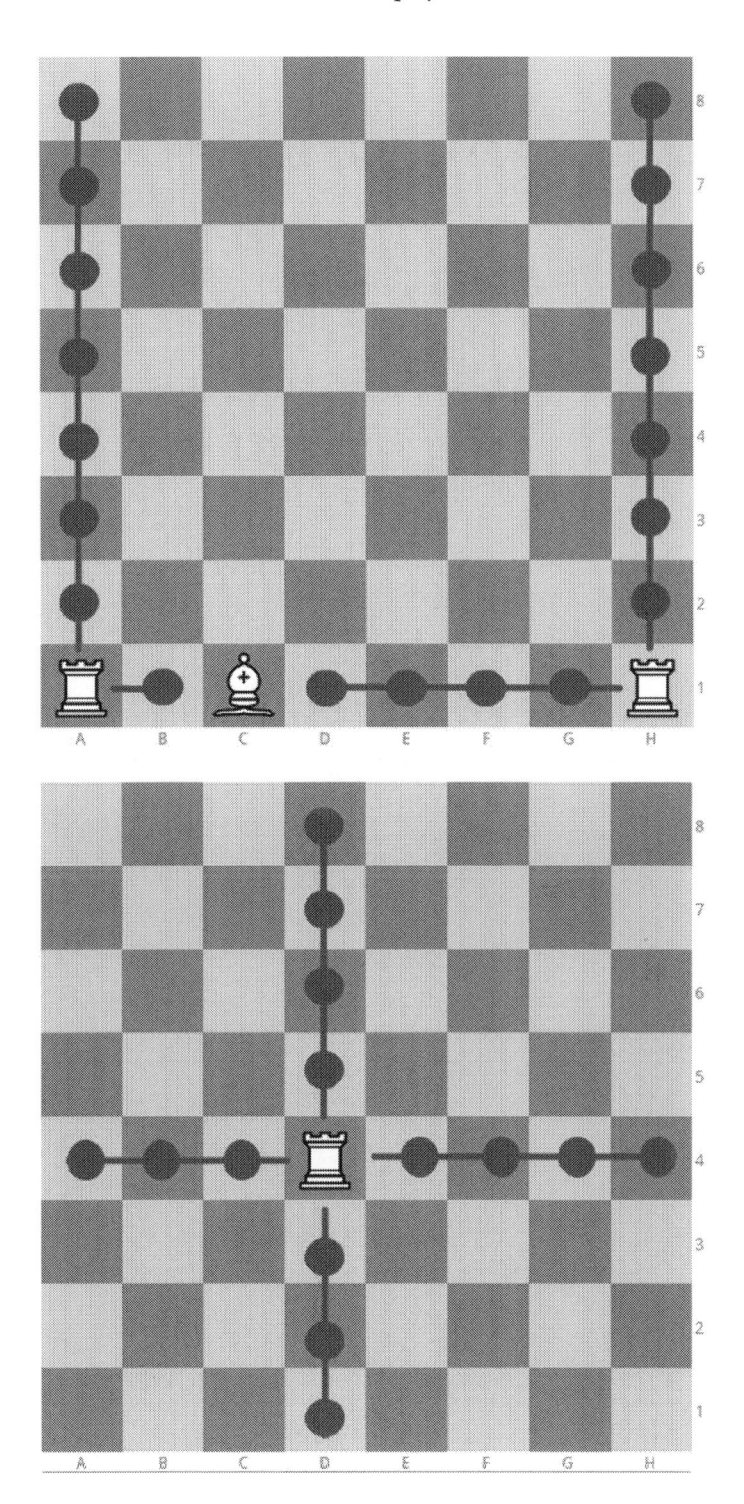

How to play

17

The **knight** is the piece that is the exception to the rule. A knight can jump over other pieces to land on a square. Imagine a horse jumping over fences to escape and run free. That being said, the movement of the knight can be confusing. The knight moves in an 'L' shape. Two squares in one direction and then one more square at a 90-degree angle. It cannot move diagonally, it can only move up, down, left or right. So for example, it could move two squares up and then one square right. The fact that a knight can jump over pieces makes it a very valuable piece in the game.

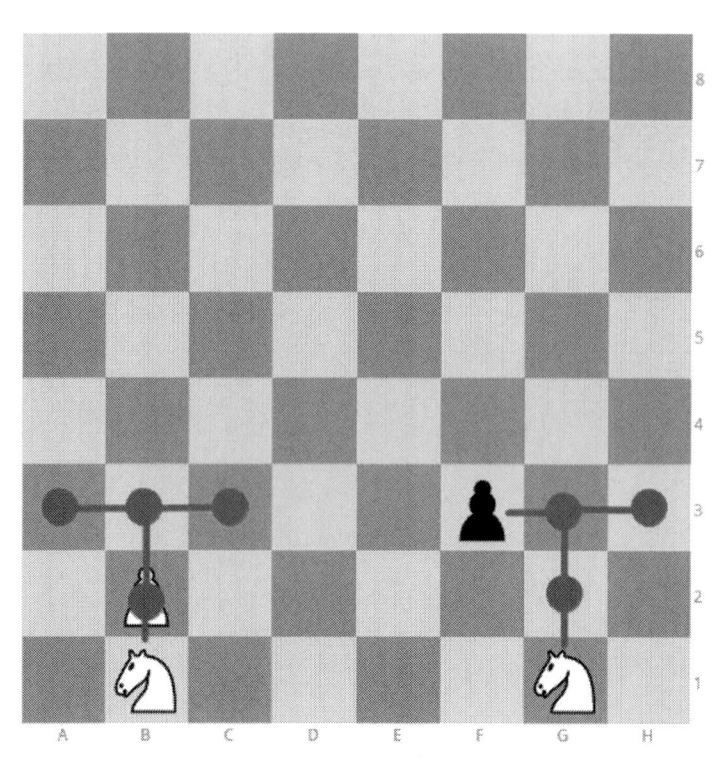

How to play

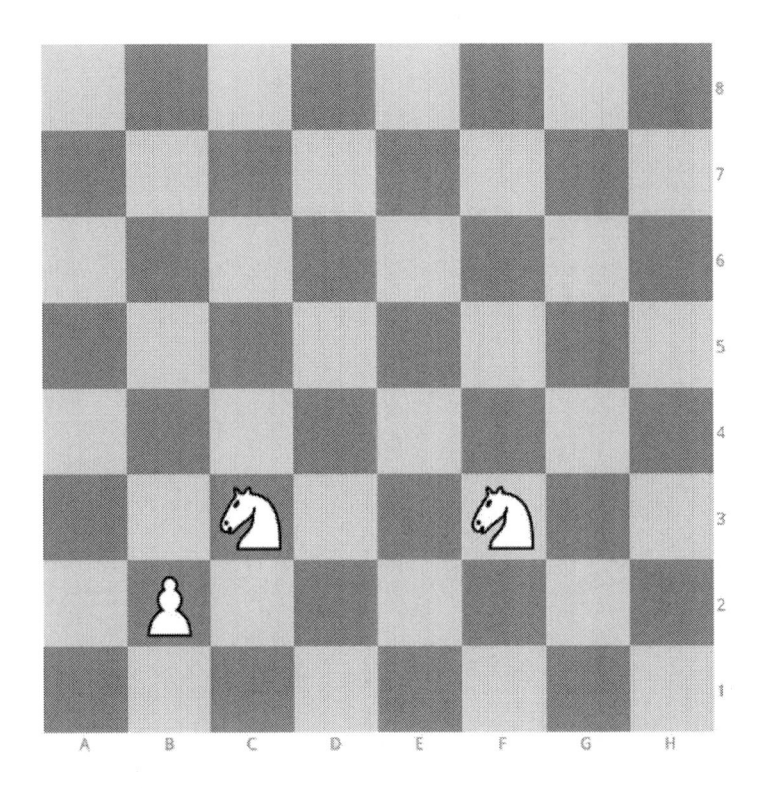

The **bishop** can only move diagonally. Like the rook, it can move in its direction for as many spaces as you want as long as there is nothing blocking it. An interesting thing to note about the bishop is that you will have one that starts on a white square and one that starts on a black square. The respective bishops will always stay on these colors, this can be valuable knowledge when attacking your opposing player, or when they are attacking you.

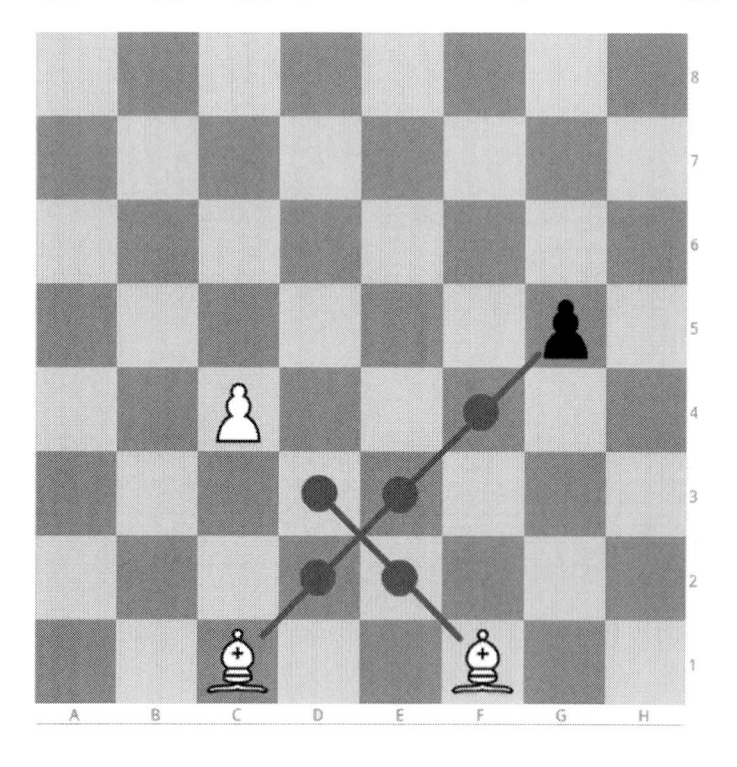

How to play

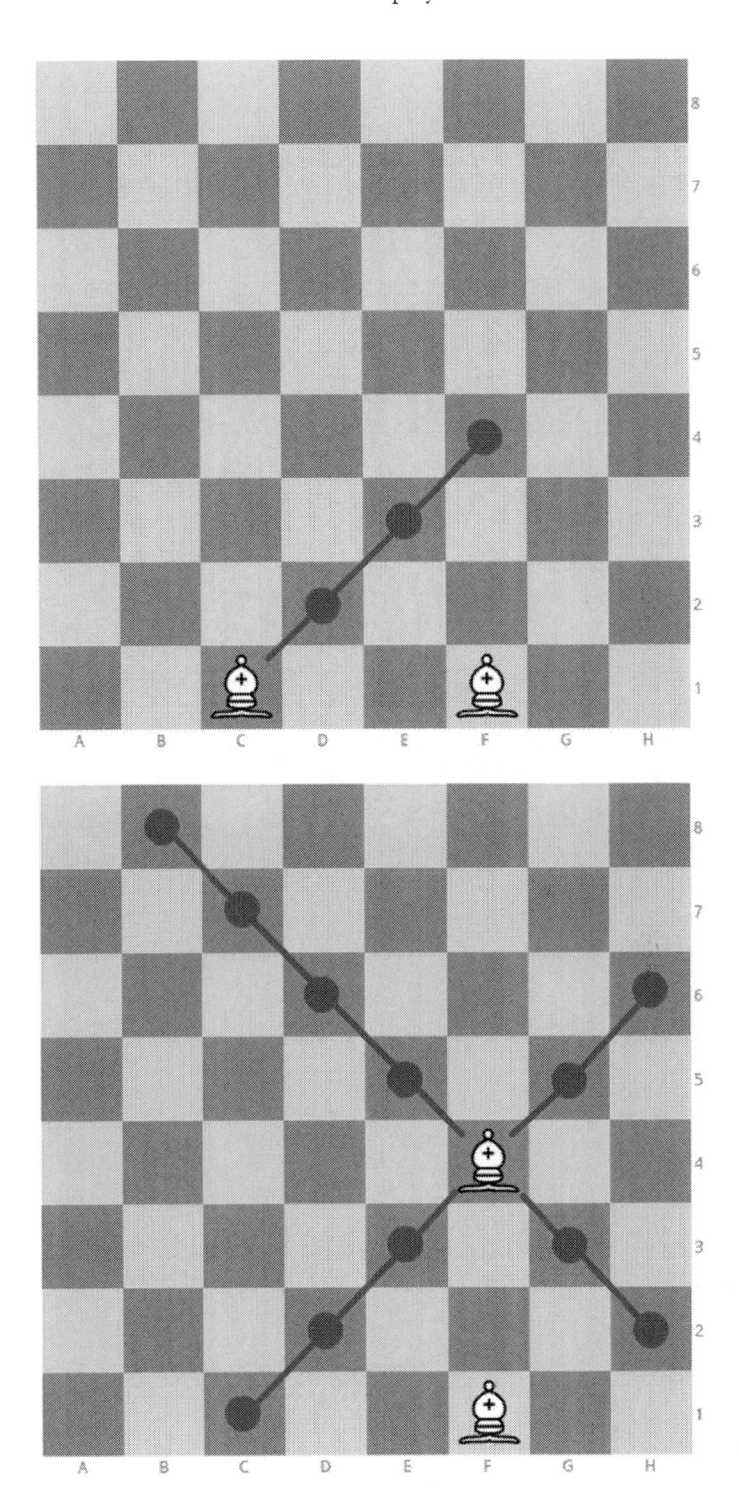

The **Queen** will be one of your most important pieces in the game. She can move in any direction, and like the bishop and rook, can move as many spaces as you want as long as she is not blocked.

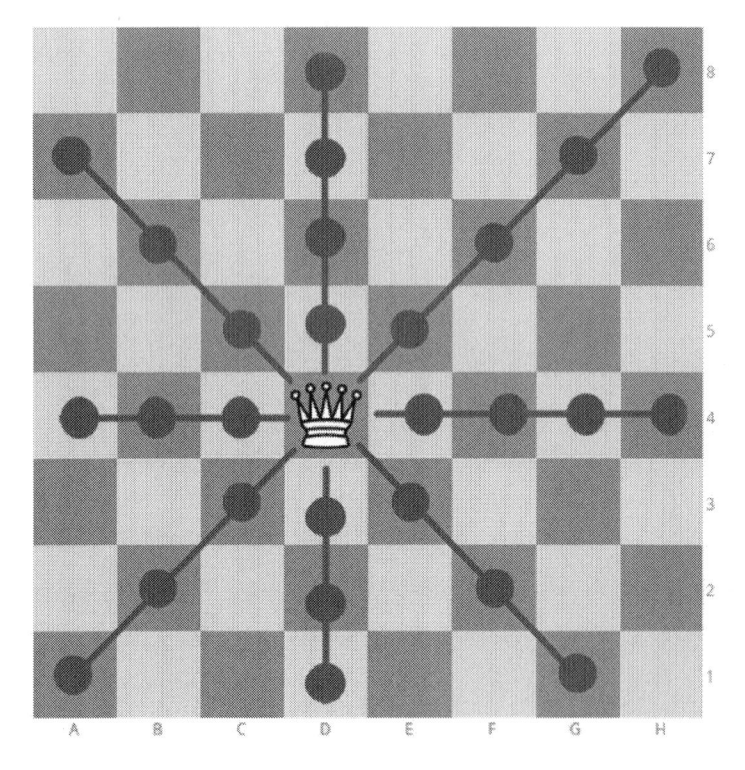

The **King** is the piece you will protect throughout the game while trying to capture the king of the opponent. As the king will not stray far from your back line of defenses, it is comforting to know that he can only move one space at a time. Like the queen, he can move in any direction, but that move is limited to one square.

How to play

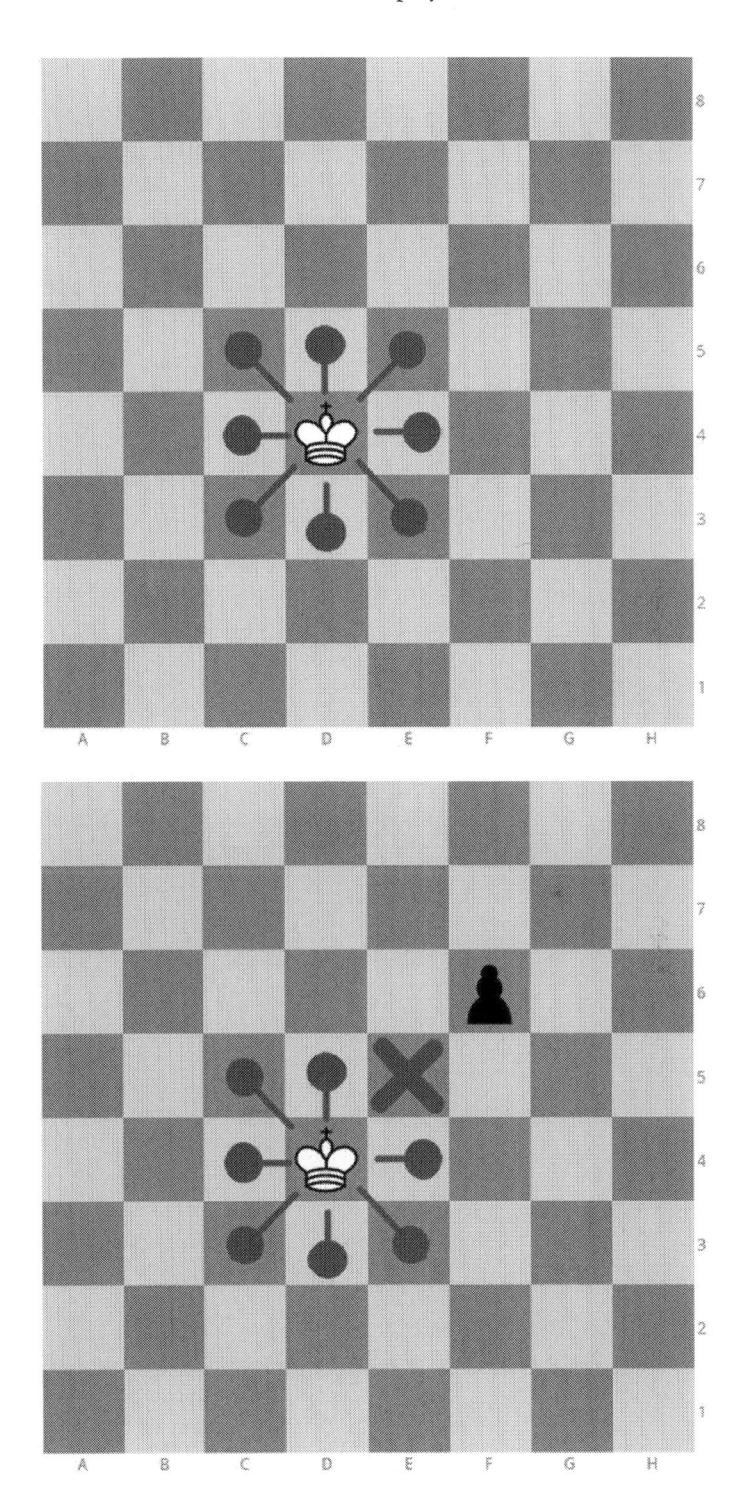

Pieces can only move in one direction at a time (with the exception of the knight which can only perform one 'L' shape move at a time). When a piece has moved in a certain direction, then their turn is over. For example, a queen cannot move two spaces forward, then one space right and the one space backward. Once the forward move has been made then her move will be over.

Additional moves

Take the time to familiarize yourself with the basic moves above, and when you come to play your first game, perhaps play the game with only those moves. This makes the gameplay less overwhelming for younger players to figure out. If you feel confident with these moves and would like to know some additional moves in the game of chess, then read on. If you would like to practice theses moves first then move on to the rules and come back to this section after you have a couple of games under your belt.

Promotion is what happens when a pawn reaches the other side of the board. While pawns often become stuck or are sacrificed during the game, there is a small chance of them making their way to the other side of the board. Often this would happen later in a game, if at all. When a pawn reaches the other side of the board it transforms into any piece you wish. Usually, this would be a queen, though sometimes it would make sense to transform to a lower piece if it can aid you better positionally. There will be times where your queen is still in play and so you

How to play

will not have the option of making a direct swap for a piece that has already been captured. If that is the case then you can use another piece, or perhaps a token of some sort, as long as both players are aware of what the piece or token represents. Promotion can turn mere pawns into game winning pieces.

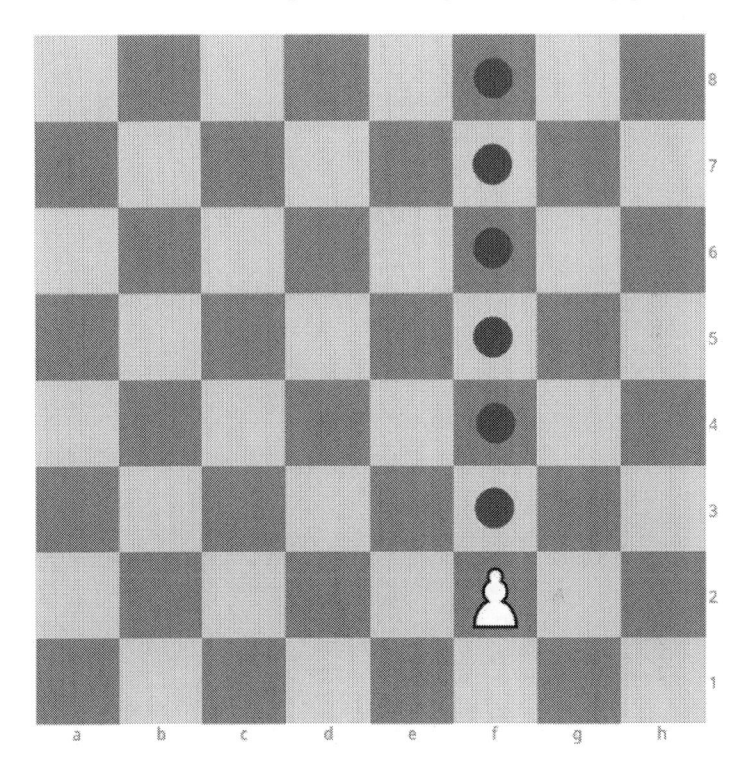

How to Play Chess

How to play

En Passant translates from French to 'in passing' and is another move which directly relates to pawns. If the movement of pawns was not already confusing enough then this rule will add some complexity to their play within the game. If a pawn moves two spaces (as it can only do on its first move) and lands beside a pawn of the opposing color, then the opposing player can choose to capture that pawn as if it had only moved one square. To do this it moves diagonally onto the square the first pawn would have moved onto had it only moved one space and the captured pawn is removed. There is one catch. The pawn that has moved two spaces must be captured immediately on the opponent's next move or the chance is lost. Confusing, but kind of fun, right?

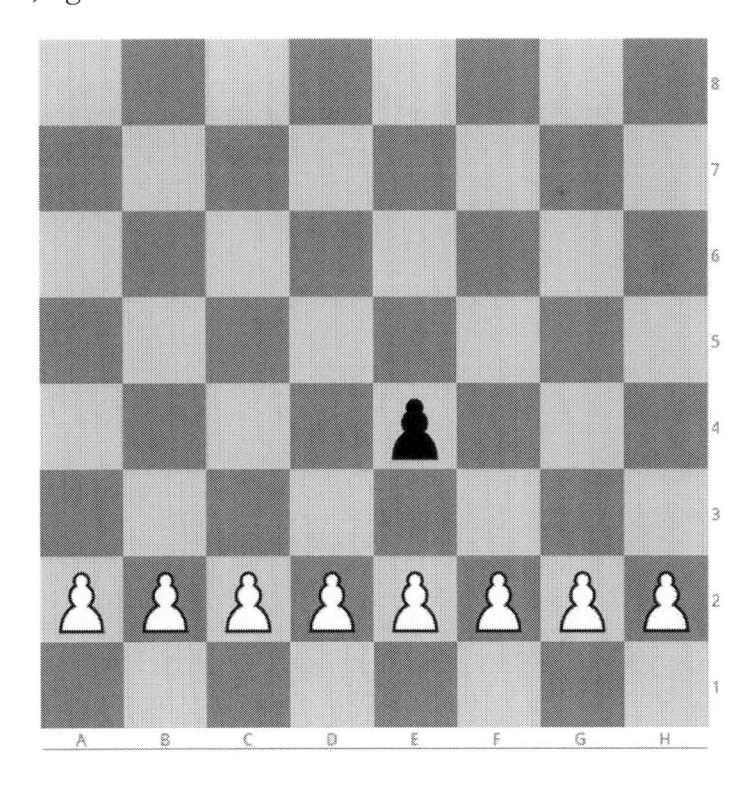

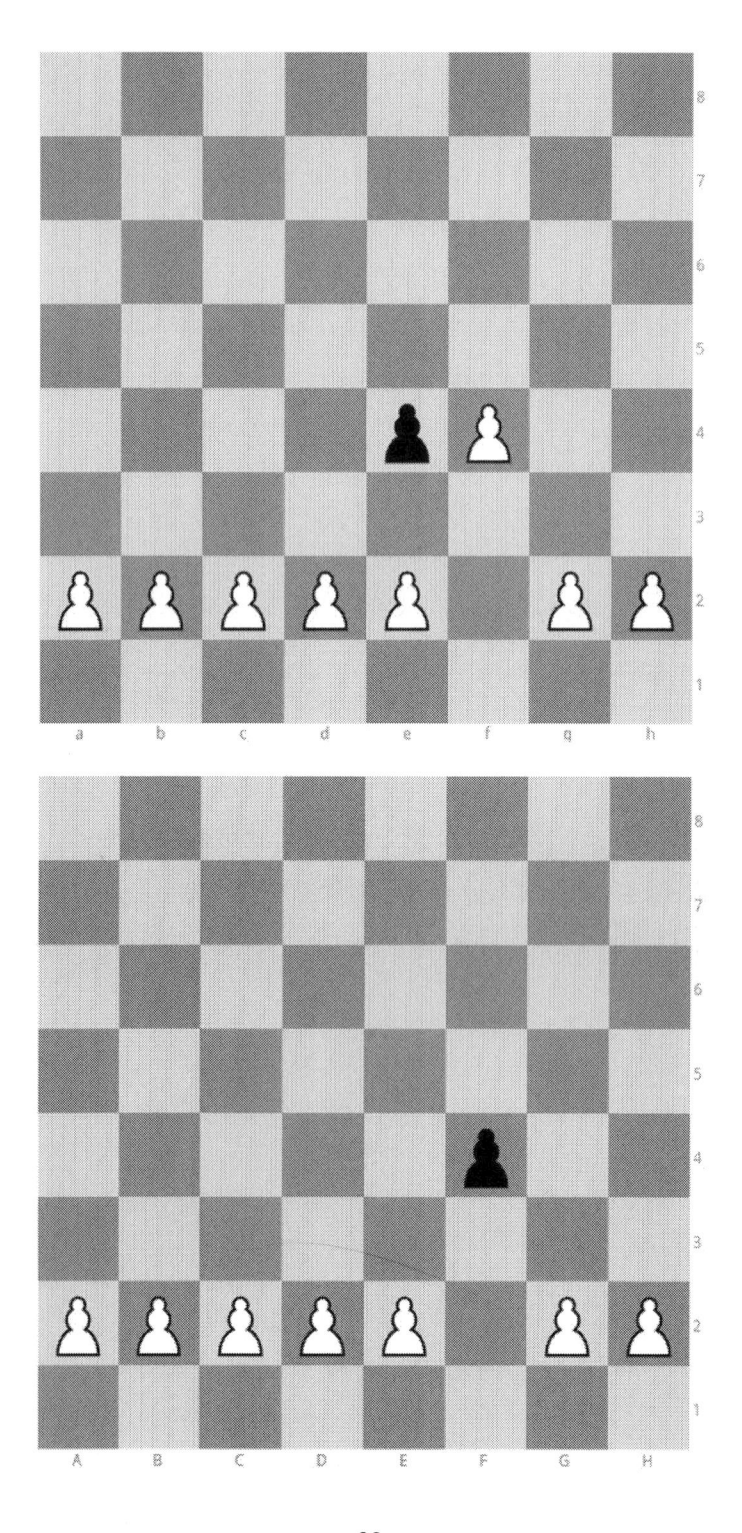

How to Play Chess

How to play

Castling can only happen if the king and the rook involved have not yet moved. Castling is the only move in chess where you move two pieces at the same time; your king and a rook. The move can only happen when there are no pieces between your king and one of your rooks and can be done with either of your rooks. This move can only be done once. The move helps to get one of your rooks out of the corner while moving your king into a safer position. To castle, you move your king two spaces towards your rook and then move the rook to the opposite side of your king. You cannot castle if it would put your king in check (see rules below) or if your king moves to a square which would put the king in check.

Castling on the left side

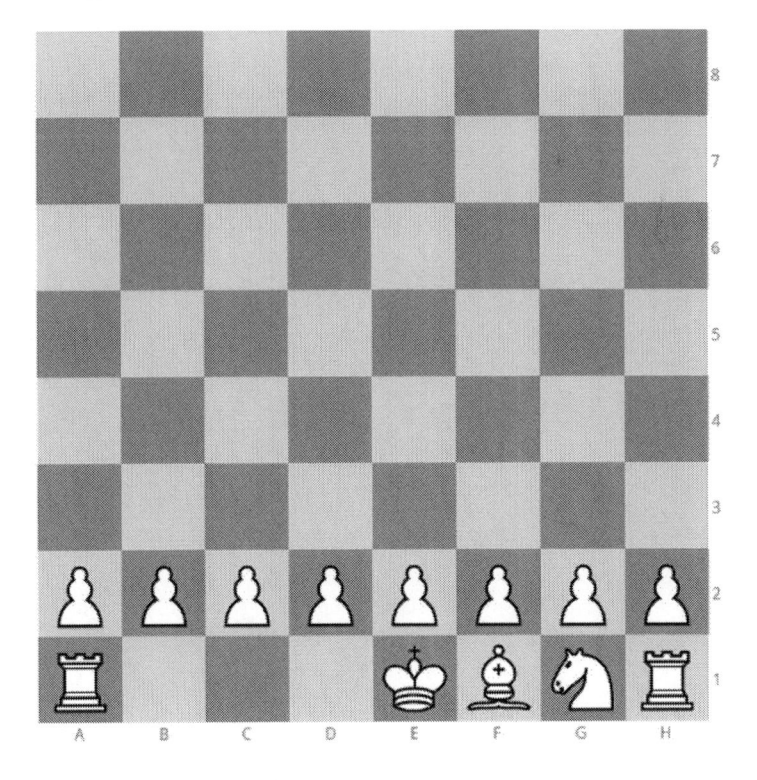

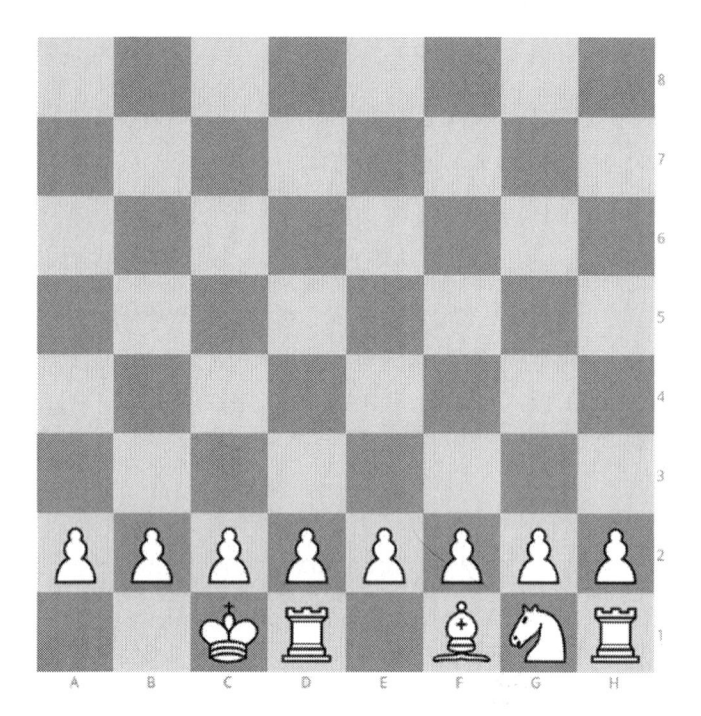

How to Play Chess

Or Castling on the right side

How to play

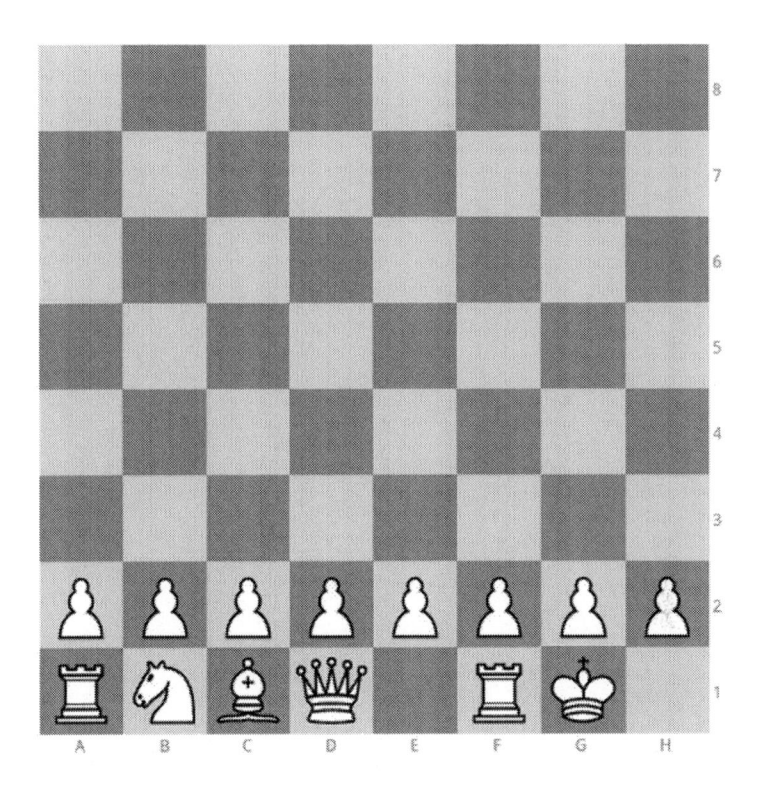

Castling that cannot be completed due to being in check or passing through check

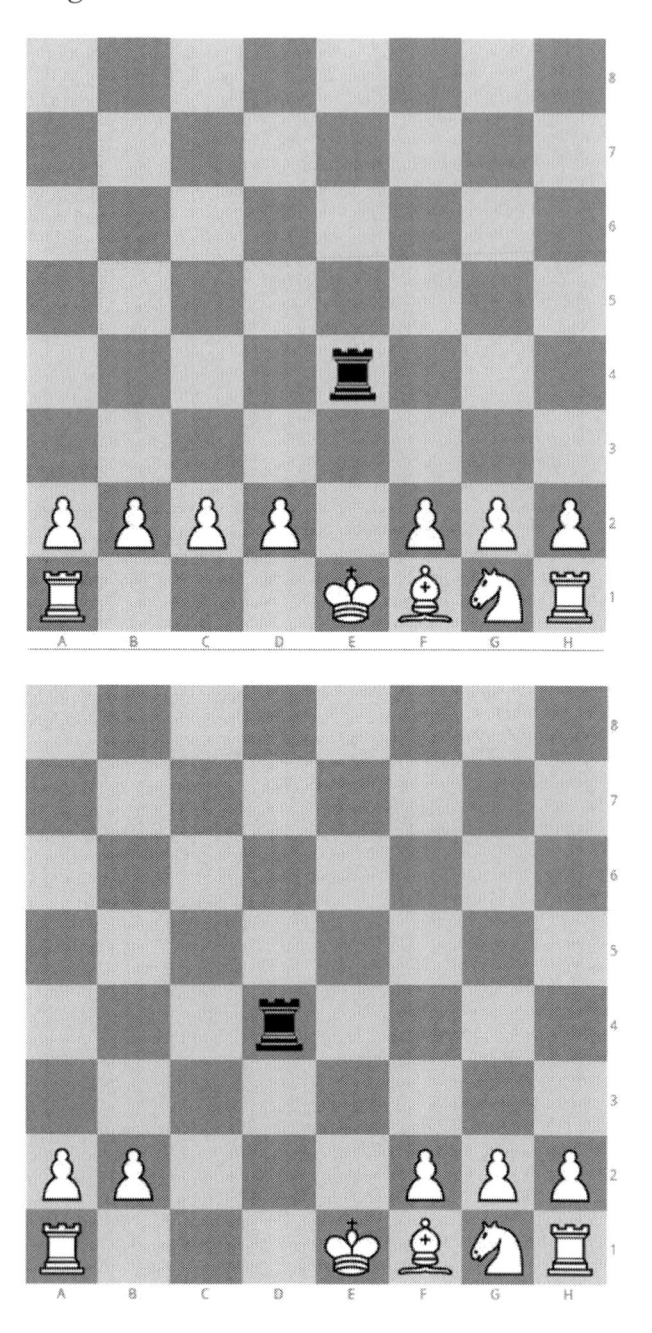

Rules

Check. One of the most important words in chess. The purpose of chess is to put the opponent's king in such a position that they cannot make a move without the king being captured. When a piece is moved into a position that would allow them to capture the opponent's king on the next move, the king is said to be in check. It is traditional for the player threatening the king to say 'check' to their opponent. The opponent now has three options to get out of check. They can move their king to a square where they are no longer in check. They can capture the piece which is threatening their king. They can place one of their pieces between the threatening piece and their king (knights cannot be blocked as they can jump over pieces).

How to Play Chess

Scenario 1:

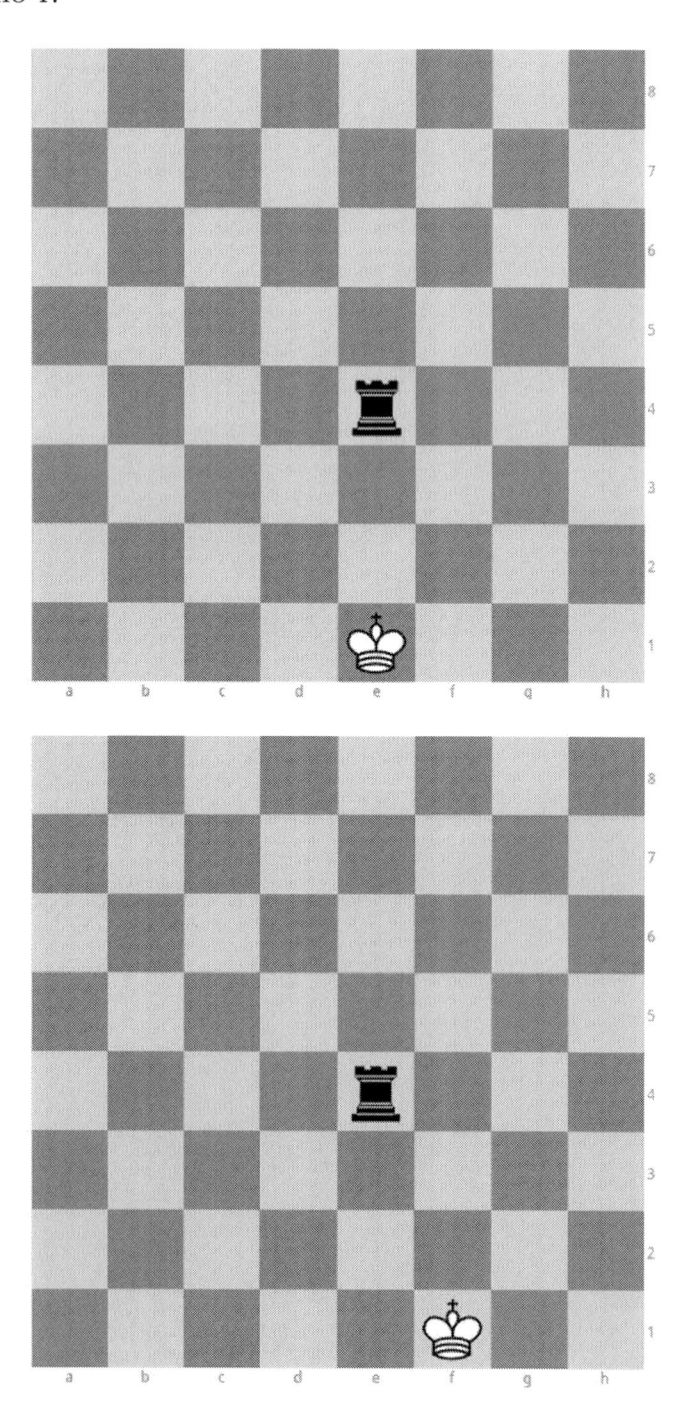

How to play

Scenario 2:

Scenario 3:

Checkmate. When checkmate occurs then the game is over. If a king is put in check and cannot evade being in check with one of the three options detailed above then it is deemed to be checkmate and the game is over. It is traditional for the attacking player to announce 'checkmate' when this occurs.

Draws. Though not common in the game of chess, it is possible for the game to end in a draw and there are five ways this could happen.

1. A stalemate is reached on the board where it is one player's turn to move, and while they are not yet in check, there are no legal moves to be made.

2. The players simply agree to stop playing and deem the match a draw.

3. There are not enough pieces on the board to force a checkmate. An example of this would be when one player is left with a king and the other is left with a king and a bishop.

4. If the exact position of pieces on the board is repeated three times then a player can announce a draw.

5. If fifty consecutive moves have been made where neither a pawn has been moved or a piece has been captured than the game is deemed to be a draw.

Touch-move (applies to tournaments though not always in friendly games). If a player touches a piece on the board then they have to move that piece. The move then ends when the player lets go of that piece. If a player wishes to adjust a piece then they must announce that before touching the piece.

How to start

The player who is in control of the white pieces always starts. The player will start by making any legal move.

How to win

To win the game you must checkmate your opponent. When this happens, we do not capture the king but end the game one move before capture.

Note you cannot check or checkmate your opponent while you yourself are in check.

Chapter 3
Basic Strategies

Protect Your King

The king is the most valuable of all of your pieces, if he is threatened then the game could be over very quickly. Make sure that you have multiple lines of defense protecting your king while at the same time using the pieces at your disposal to threaten the opposing king. Often you will find that your pieces can do both.

Castling early is an effective way of protecting your king and moving your king towards a corner of the board is also a good idea. It does not matter how close you are to capturing your opponent's king if they are closer to capturing yours. Keep your king safe at all costs.

Do Not Give Away Pieces

We generally rank the pieces on the board in this order: king, queen, rook, bishop/knight, and pawn. The king is infinitely valuable, for if he is captured then the game is over.

We do not want to give our pieces away without gaining something in return. Allowing a pawn to be captured may not seem like the end of the world, but allowing capture one-by-one can quickly end our game.

Pieces, when threatened, can be move or be backed up by other pieces. For example, an opposing bishop moves onto a square where it will capture our knight on its next move. We move our queen so that when our knight is captured we can use our queen to capture the bishop. We have traded off our pieces and those pieces have the same worth so the game remains even.

When the game is even it is generally a good idea to trade off pieces which are worth less than your opponents. If we allow them to capture our pawn so that we can then capture their rook, then we would be ahead in the game. We want to stop the opposite from happening.

If we are in the midst of a game where we are ahead, then it makes sense for us to trade off pieces of equal value.

Another time where it would make sense for us to allow a piece to be captured would be when it would give us a better position on the board. If we can sacrifice a piece so we can checkmate our opponent, then we will do it. If we can sacrifice a piece so that we can put the opponent in check with the eventual goal of checkmate then it may be worth doing. There may even be times where sacrificing a piece has no immediate benefit until later in the game, but this knowledge will not be apparent to the beginner player.

When first delving into the game of chess it is standard practice to protect your pieces and only trade when you are in control of the game. Remember the more pieces you lose, the harder and harder it will be to win the game and the value of the pieces on the board means nothing when checkmate is achieved.

Basic Strategies

Control the Center of The Board

It is typical for the opposing king to be contained to the other side of the board throughout most of the game and so out strategy should be to eventually get our pieces over to that side of the board. In the early game, though, we cannot do that without first making our way through the center of the board. The center of the board will be where most of the gameplay takes place.

If you can control the center of the board then you will have more room and freedom to move your pieces around the board while stifling you opponent. Keep track of the line of sight of your pieces and your opponents. Can you block your opponent's pieces? Where are they moving their pieces to? Can you set traps for your opponent?

Take the time to plan a move or two ahead and think about what your opponent is planning. If you can begin to control the center then you are on your way to winning the game.

Use All of Your Pieces

If your pieces are sitting back on the first two rows doing nothing then you may as well not have them in the game. Against a good player, you will not win with only one or two pieces. Your pieces should be used to serve a purpose. Are they protecting your king? Are they attacking your opponent?

Of course, at the start of the game, it will take some time to move all of your pieces into these desired positions, but it is the player who can get these pieces into position first that will have the advantage.

Formulate a plan and decide what your pieces are to be used for. Which ones will offer protection? Which ones will be used for attack? Which pieces are to be sacrificed? You will not know the answer to these questions until the game is underway.

Take the time to get to know the pieces and your opponent. Discover how they can work together. Have a plan for each one. Setting a trap or pouncing on your opponent at the right time will give you the same rush that the players throughout the years and geographical locations have experienced.

Get Better

There are three great ways to get better: play, study and have fun.

Find a local chess club or even a player or two in your area, friend group or family. It is only by playing the game that you will improve. Be sure to play against players who are better than you, you will lose a lot at first, but it is only by losing that you can find the weakness in your game. Watch them as they play, discover the moves that have and how they can be applied to your own game. The more you play, the better you will get and the more you will begin to win.

Find more literature on chess. This book is only a beginners guide. There are thousands of books, magazines, and websites to discover that will teach you more about chess. Talk to other players about strategies and moves. Watch them play against each other or in tournaments. Download a chess game and practice against a computational mind.

The most important thing you can do, though, is having fun. If you are not having fun, you will never be the player you are destined to be. If chess is boring, then it is not for you. Find ways to make chess fun, play in the games or tournaments that are fun for you, take a break when it all becomes too much. Put fun first and the rest will come together.

Chapter 4
Beginner strategies

The Opening

In chess, we call the start of the game, the first few moves, the opening. This is the most important part of the game as this sets us up for the remainder of our encounter. If we can gain an advantage at the very beginning then chances are we can continue this through to the end. So what can we do in the beginning to give us this advantage? With a lot of chess play, we can begin to become familiar with what works and what does not work. By studying players who are better than us we can begin to see patterns in their opening games.

The possible opening moves have been studied for years. The seemingly infinite number of combinations have been whittled down into distinct approaches, with some being named for the players who developed them. Take some to go search out the different opening combinations for both black and white pieces.

In our opening we have their basic goals:

- Develop our pieces

- Control the center

- Protect our king

As white, one of our best opening moves is to develop the pawn above our king. By moving this forward two spaces, we begin to control the center of the board, we allow space for our bishop and queen to move out of the back row and we move a step closer to castling. Hey, we just killed three birds with one stone. Bringing out our kingside knight next can help to further control the center of the board, and also take us a step closer to castling. Each of our moves should serve a purpose, and beware for each of your opponents moves should serve a purpose too. The standard third move in this sequence is to bring out your bishop and then to castle. This is an excellent beginner, and advanced, opening.

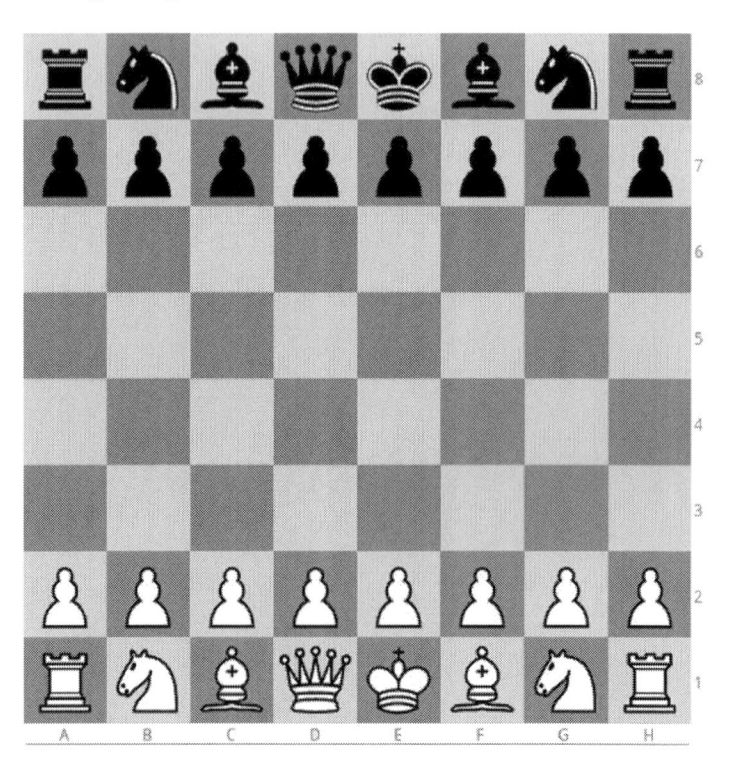

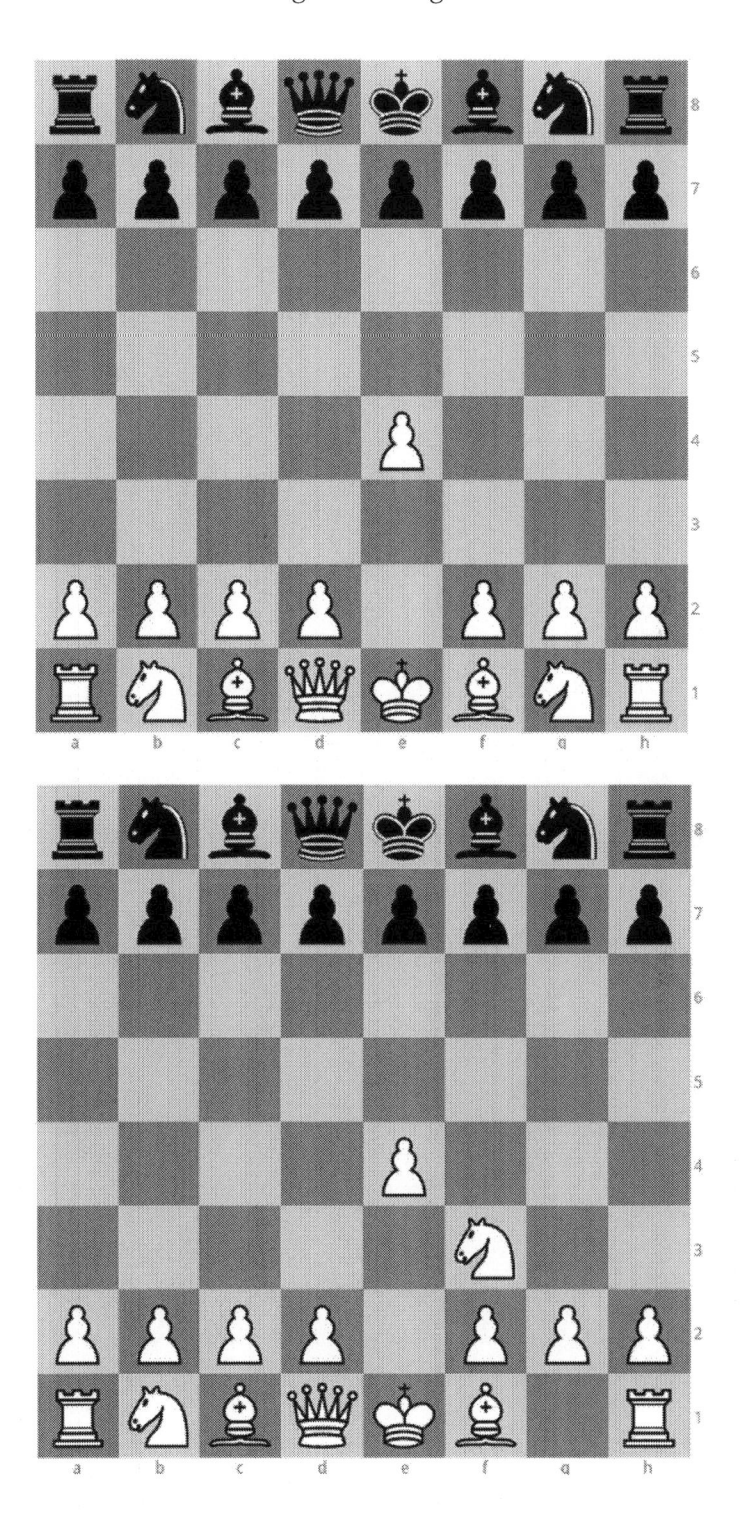

Beginner strategies

How to Play Chess

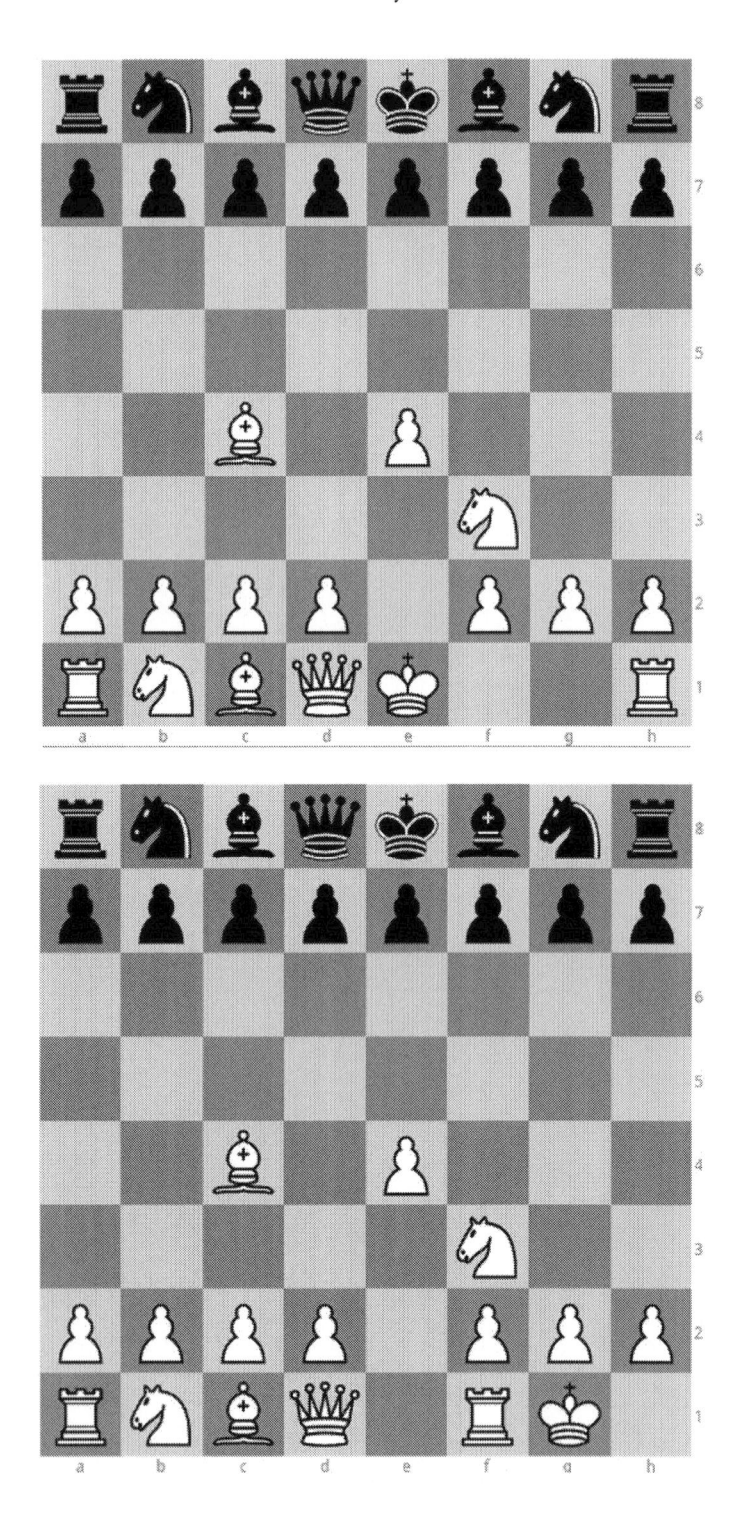

The Game

You have opened your game you may find yourself with this question: *now what?* There are many things to think about and plan for at this stage:

- Try to place each piece to its best square. Your pieces should not be moved back and forth, especially in the opening stages. Place each piece where it will help with your attack, help to solidify your defenses or both. Get your pieces off their starting squares and into play. Generally, the player who is able to do this quickest will have the advantage in the game.

- Protect your king. Castling is a great way to do this if your defense line of paws at either side is unbreached and unmoved. Moving the king towards the corner and away from obvious attacks will help your game. If you limit the number of ways the opponent pieces can attack your king and set up a line of defense between those pieces and your king then you are going to increase the number of moves it will take for your opponent to checkmate you.

- Watch your pawns. While in the early game you will want to advance your central pawns to help control the center of the board, it is not great practice to advance all of your pawns. One obvious reason not to do this is to protect your king on one side of the board. Since pawns can never move backward, advanced pawns can become easy pickings for an advanced player and can allow opening through which your opponent can develop and attack.

- Take the initiative. If you can develop a piece while threatening another piece then you will limit the moves of your opponent. If you can force an opponent to move a piece backward, or to move an established game piece then you can stall the attack and make them rethink their plan.

- Plan a move or two ahead. When you are moving a piece, take the time to think about what your next move will be, then your next, and then your next. It is of no use to move a piece just for the sake of it, each move should be part of a bigger plan.

- Study your opponent's move. When learning chess you will play against complete novices, beginners, advanced players and perhaps even masters and grandmasters (good luck!). For the average chess player, a move means soothing. After your opponent moves a piece, take the time to ask why? Why did they move *that* piece? Why did they move that piece *there*? What is their plan? Look for pieces they are threatening. Look for sacrifices they can make. Look for an attack on your king. Look two or three moves ahead for this too.

- Sacrifice. There will be many times where sacrificing a piece can make sense. Can you sacrifice a weaker piece for a stronger one? Can you sacrifice a piece for another of equal value when you are ahead in the game? Will sacrificing a piece give you a better board position? Can a sacrifice lead to check or even checkmate? Do not be afraid to lose your pieces, in

Beginner strategies

chess you will lose many pieces in a game, the secret is to make it count.

- Threatening two pieces. A great move as a beginner is to be able to threaten two pieces at the same time without your piece being threatened. For example, your opponent has a brook and a knight close together on the board. You are able to move up a pawn and threaten both at the same time (on your next move you could capture either of them). Your opponent now has a choice; they can either leave both pieces where they are and allow you to capture either or they could decide which piece they wish to keep and move that one away allowing you to capture the other on your next move. Of course, there are other ways for your opponent to get out of this situation, but this is a scenario to look out for in your games.

- Threatening a piece while putting the opponent king in check. If you can move a piece into position so that it threatens an opponent piece which putting the opponent king in check then you will find yourself smiling inside. Of course, this only works if your opponent is unable to immediately capture your piece. If you are able to maneuver yourself into this position you force your opponent to move or protect your king and you are left free to capture the threatened piece.

- Be adaptable. You have your plan, it is going well, you are a few moves from checkmating your opponent, or perhaps you are only beginning your attack. Then disaster strikes! One of your pieces is captured or your opponent throws in a confusing move. Now you cannot continue your amazing plan. Fear not for the great chess player will adapt and try a new plan, maybe they started out with three of four plans for just such a situation. No matter what happens a great chess player will be able to adapt to whatever happens during the game.

- Checkmate. You cannot checkmate your opponent with just one piece, so when you are building you attack try to focus on which pieces work well together and how you are going to utilize them in your plan for attack.

- Learn patterns. Our brains are hardwired to recognize patterns and the more you play chess the more your brain will learn these patterns instinctively. Play as many games as you can and soon you will begin to recognize what your opponent is doing without even thinking about it and be able to plan your attack with instinct.

- Look for weakness. I any chess game there will be some weakness from your opponent, the key is to be able to exploit this through your play. Look for a stray pawn, an unprotected piece or ab easy line of attack. How do I do this? The answer is to play as many games as possible. At the beginning, you will find that the weaknesses in your own game are exploited with ease. Soon you will be able to protect from these attacks as your game improves and then as you improve further you will find yourself finding a weakness in your opponents game.

- Play. This point backs up every point on the list so far. The best way to improve your game, the best beginner strategy, the best expert strategy, the best strategy of all is to practice, practice, practice. Play, play, play!

The Endgame

You have had a strong opening, your game is going well, now is the time to finish the game. But how? Here are some of the things that we need to know to succeed late in the game, through to winning.

- Learn to checkmate. You have made it this far. Well done. Now you need to finish off your opponent before they can finish off you. There are fewer pieces on the board, making it easier to attack. The easiest way to checkmate your opponent is to have your queen still in play, failing that then two rooks make for an easy checkmate too. If you do not have these pieces then it becomes harder and harder, but still possible. Try to keep this in mind as you are playing the game. The common way to checkmate is to start by putting the opposing king in check. This puts you on the front foot and your opponent on the back foot. Visualize the end position you wish to achieve to checkmate your opponent and work back in your mind from there. As always, the more you play, the more you will familiarize yourself with strategies for checkmating your opponent.

- Push your pawns. This is where your pawns start to become more and more valuable. As the game goes on, the number of pieces that each player owns will become less and less and so each piece the player holds becomes more valuable than it was at the start of the game. The board is also more open and free and so it is time to advance your pawns, either in attack or with the goal of getting them to the other side of the board for promotion. In a game with few pieces, a pawn promoted to a queen will be the deciding factor.

- The king is alive. The pieces are few, so now it is time to bring any remaining pieces into play. While it is good practice to protect your king, there are times, especially at the end of a game, where bringing your king into attacking play will be invaluable. There will even be times where you will have to attack with your king to checkmate your opponent.

- Piece for piece. The game is coming to an end, the pieces are few, but you are ahead by a piece or two, or in the value of the pieces. If you are able to trade pieces until your opponents pieces are all gone, while still leaving yourself with enough pieces to checkmate your opponent then the win will be easy.

- Play often. Again I cannot stress enough the importance of playing as much as you are able to. There you play, the better you will get. It really is as simple as that.

Chapter 5
Chess: the players and the changes

The new era: Magnus Carlsen

Magnus Carlsen was born in November, 1990 and became a chess grandmaster at the young age of thirteen. He is a Norwegian superstar and one of the most prodigious players ever in the game of chess. He is currently the highest ever rated chess player. Let that sink in. Magnus Carlsen, at sixteen years old, is the highest rated player in the history of chess.

We are in the midst of the 'Magnus Carlsen Era' and where he goes from here is anybody's guess. He became World Champion at age 23 and is a fashion model. Carlsen's game is well rounded, showcases blistering attacks and has an unlimited defines arsenal. He is able to understand the position of the game at a computer like level and calculate moves well into the endgame. There is little doubt that he will continue to wow the chess world for many years to come.

Carlsen's style of play is noted for his natural ability to make moves, the moves occur to him naturally, and his ability to force opponents into more mistakes than any other player is able to do. Carlsen has helped to make chess more fashionable, he is also been coached by Garry Kasparov.

The celebrities: Garry Kasparov and Bobby Fisher

Bobby Fisher learned the rules of chess at six years old and as he played through his childhood years he became 'naturally good' (practice makes perfect). He became grandmaster at the age of fifteen, setting the record at the time. Into the early 1970s, Fisher defeated the Soviet greats and became world champion, before disappearing from the chess world in 1975.

The chess world lacked a superstar until ten years later when Garry Kasparov appeared on the scene. Kasparov became the youngest chess champion of the time and dominated the chess world for nearly twenty-two years. His rating was the highest in history until a young Norwegian player came along.

Both of these men stand as the universal faces of chess and are considered the most famous chess champions of all time.

The original champion: Willian Steinitz

Austrian-American William Steinitz was the very first chess champion after defeating Johannes Zukertort in 1886 and has contributed enormously to the game of chess. His biggest contribution was the strategic understanding of the game. Before Steinitz, the style of play was romantic and big. Fierce attacks and a 'style over outcome' mentality. Steinitz's style of play focused more on the structure of his pawn line and his active bishops and knights. Attacks were only launched after careful preparation and positioning. At first, his style was labeled as cowardly, but he is now known as the father of modern chess.

Time for a change

In the early 1800s, games of chess would often last more than fourteen hours (longer than the Superbowl!) and weaker opponents would often try to outlast and tire their opponents. In 1861 the first chess timers were invented, using hourglasses filled with sand. This later gave way to 'tumbling' clocks which would start one clock running at the moment the other on stopped. The first electronic clocks came in 1964, giving a more accurate timing system.

The pieces we all know and love

Englishman Howard Staunton was the greatest chess player in the world from 1843 to 1851. He was a passionate promoter of the game and advocated specifically for chess piece style. The pieces we commonly use today were designed by a chess journalist and feature simple design with easy piece recognition. They have become known as 'Staunton' pieces and are the standard pieces used around the world.

Chapter 6
Checkmate: the conclusion

The king is threatened and captured; the game is over.

Chess has come a long way since its humble beginnings, hundreds of years ago in India. Now a game played around the world by king and pauper alike, a popular cultural staple and a way for friends and enemies alike to some together over a board and settle differences. The rules have changed many times, but the popularity of chess today would suggest that the final stage of chess is upon us.

Chess has been a big part of international disputes, the games between Russia and the USA coming at time when tensions were high, providing a national sense of togetherness and camaraderie that would ripple across the country. What part has chess played in the shaping of nations?

Now the torch has been passed onto you. You have made it this far, you are either a chess player or do not like to leave a book unfinished. Take up your board and start your first game, your tenth game, your thousandth game. Time is your friend. Take the time to get to know the pieces, all will be valuable in your attack and defense. Take the time to find people to play against. Join a local club or star your own. Take the time to study the great players of the past, the great players of the present, the strategies, the moves, the combinations, the openings, the checkmates, the pincer moves, the pins, the sneaky attacks, the solid defenses and your own play.

When you feel ready, enter a tournament, this will open your eyes to a new style of play and intensity. Gain a rating and get a feel for where your game is strong and where your game is weak. Play, play, play and when you have done that, play some more.

Perhaps you will be the new Bobby Fisher, Garry Kasparov or Magnus Carlsen. Are you the newest World Champion or Grandmaster? There is only one way to find out.

Good luck!

Thank You!

I hope you enjoyed this book as much as I've enjoyed writing it! If you would please take 20 seconds of your time to review this book, it would mean so much to me, to hear how you've enjoyed it.

Leave a Review here:

https://www.amazon.com/review/create-review/ref=cm_cr_arp_d_wr_but_rgt?ie=UTF8&channel=reviews-product&asin=B06VWS35TR#

Printed by Amazon Italia Logistica S.r.l.
Torrazza Piemonte (TO), Italy

Printed in Great Britain
by Amazon

Rocke, Michael, *Forbidden Friendships*, 1997.
Romans Grecs et Latin, Gallimard, 1958.
Rouse, W.H.D., Homer's *The Iliad*, 1938.
Thucydides, *The Peloponnesian War,* Penguin Classics.
Vernant, Jean-Pierre, *Mortals and Immortals*, 1991.
Virgil, *The Aeneid*, Everyman's Library, Knopf, 1907.
Wikipedia: Research today is impossible without the aid of this monument.
Worthington, Ian, *Philip II of Macedonia*, 2008.
Xenophon, *A History of My Time*s, Penguin Classics.
Xenophon, *The Persian Expedition*, 1949.

All pictures are from Wikipedia, a monument to its creator.

I would be very grateful to have your comments:
mbhone@gmail.com

that when a man grows old he should keep a distance from boys, but in his heart he knows that the only alternative to loving a boy is simply to cease to exist.

OTHER SOURCES

Aldrich, Robert, *Who's Who in Gay and Lesbian History*, 2001.
Aristophanes, Bantam Drama, 1962.
Barber, Stanley, *Alexandros*, 2010.
Bradford, Ernle, *Thermopylae*, 1980.
Bury and Meiggs, *A History of Greece*, 1975.
Calimach, Andrew, *Lover's Legends*, 2002.
Cartledge, Paul, *Alexander the Great*, 2004.
Cartledge, Paul, *Sparta and Lakonia*, 1979.
Cartledge, Paul, *The Spartans*, 2002.
Cartledge, Paul, *Thermopylae*, 2006.
Ceram, C.W., *Gods, Graves and Scholars*, 1951.
Davidson, James, *Courtesans and Fishcakes*, 1998.
Davidson, James, *The Greeks and Greek Love*, 2007.
Dover K.J. *Greek Homosexuality*, 1978
Everitt, Anthony, *Hadrian*, 2009.
Fagles, Robert, *The Iliad*, 1990.
Graves, Robert, *Greek Myths*, 1955.
Halperin David M. *One Hundred Years of Homosexuality*, 1990
Herodotus, *The Histories*, Penguin Classics.
Hesiod and Theognis, Penguin Classics, 1973.
Hine, Daryl, *Puerilities*, 2001.
Holland, Tom, *Persian Fire*, 2005.
Hughes-Hallett, *Heroes*, 2004.
Kagan, Donald, *The Peloponnesian War*, 2003.
Lévy, Edmond, *Sparte, 1979.*
Malye, Jean, *La Véritable Histore d'Alcibiade*, 2009.
Matyszak, Philip, *The Mithridates the Great*, 2008.
Meyer, Jack, *Alcibiades*, 2009.
Opper, Thorsten, *Hadrian, Empire and Conflict*, 2008.
Peyrefitte, Roger, *Alexandre*, 1979.
Plutarch's Lives, Modern Library.
Polybius, *The Histories*.

boy-love that described the love of Orpheus for Calais, and his death at the hands of Thracian women. Mimnermus was born in Ionian Smyrna around 630 B.C. He wrote short love poems suitable for performance at drinking parties. Polyenus was a Macedonian known as a rhetorician and for his books on war strategies. Cicero was born in 106 B.C. and murdered by Mark Antony in 43 B.C. Michael Grant said it all when he wrote, ''the influence of Cicero upon the history of European literature and ideas greatly exceeds that of any other prose writer in any language.'' (For more about Cicero, see my book *Roman Homosexuality*.)

A special mention for Pindar, Theognis and Theocritus. Pindar's great love was Theoxenus of Tenodos about whom he wrote: ''Whosoever, once he has seen the rays flashing from the eyes of Theoxenus, and is not shattered by the waves of desire, has a black heart forged of a cold flame. Like wax of the sacred bees, I melt when I look at the young limbs of boys.'' He lived around 500 B.C. and celebrated the Greek victories against the Persians at Salamis and Plataea. His home in Thebes became a must for his devotees. Theognis was born around 550 B.C. His poems consist of maxims and advice as to how to live life. Fortunately, a great deal of his work has come down to us, most of which is dedicated to his beloved, the handsome Cyrnus. Theocritus was a Sicilian and lived around 270 B.C. In his 7th Idyll Aratus is passionately in love with a lad. His 12th Idyll refers to Diocles who died saving the life of Philolaus, the boy he loved, and in whose honor kissing contests were held every spring at his tomb. In his 23rd Idyll a lover commits suicide because of unrequited love, warning his beloved that one day he too will burn and weep for a cruel boy. Before hanging himself the lover kissed the doorpost from which he would attach the noose. The boy treated the corpse with disdain and went off to the gymnasium for a swim where a statue of Eros fell on him, coloring the water with his blood. In his 29th Idyll a lover warns his beloved that he too will age and his beauty will lose its freshness. He is therefore advised to show more kindness as ''you will one day be desperate for a beautiful young man's attentions.'' Although lads are often disappointing, it is impossible not to fall madly in love with them. In the 30th Idyll the poet states

Other key sources are: Athenaeus who lived in the times of Marcus Aurelius (meaning we know little about him). His *Deipnosopistae* is a banquet conversation *à la Platon* during which conversations on every possible subject took place, filling fifteen books that have come down to us. Isocrate was a student of Socrates who wrote a speech in the defense of Alcibiades. Cornelius Nepos was a Roman friend of Cicero. Most of what he wrote was lost, so what we know comes through passages of his works in the books of other historians. Andocides was implicated in the Hermes scandal and saved his skin by turning against Alcibiades in a speech that has come down to us called, what else?, *Against Alcibiades*. Lysias was extremely wealthy and contemporary with Alcibiades. He founded a new profession, logographer, which consisted of writing speeches delivered in law courts. One of his speeches was *Against Andocides*, another was *Against Alcibiades*. Diodorus Siculus who lived around 50 B.C. and wrote *Historical Library*, consisting of forty volumes. Pausanias, a Greek historian and geographer, famous for his *Description of Greece*. He was contemporary with Hadrian and Marcus Aurelius. He's noted as being someone interested in everything, careful in his writing and scrupulously honest. Simonides of Ceos was a Greek poet born about 550 B.C. Besides his poems, he added four letters to the Greek alphabet. Bion was a Greek philosopher known for his diatribes, satires and attacks on religion. He lived around 300 B.C. Ovid lived around 10 B.C. A Roman poet especially known for his Metamorphoses, one of the world's most important sources of classical mythology. Polybius was a Greek historian born in Arcadia around 200 B.C. His work describes the rise of the Roman Republic and he is known for his ideas on the separation of powers in government. Aelianus was a Roman author and teacher of rhetoric who spoke and wrote in Greek. Philemon lived to be a hundred but alas only fragments of his works remain. He must have been very popular as he won numerous victories as a poet and playwright. The Greek poet Anacreon was born in 582 B.C. and was known for his drinking songs. Eupolis lived around 430 B.C. An Athenian poet who lived and wrote during the Peloponnesian Wars. Phanocles lived during the time of Alexander the Great. He was the author of a poem on where he wrote while contemplating sea and sky. When Sparta defeated Athens in war, it did not destroy the city-state. Plutarch states that this was thanks to one of Euripides' plays, *Electra*, put on for the Spartans in Athens, a play they found so wonderful that they proclaimed that it would be barbarous to destroy a city capable of engendering men of the quality of Euripides. (The real reason was to preserve the city that had twice saved Greece from Persian victory.) Euripides was known for his love of Agathon, a youth praised for his beauty as well as for his culture, and would later become a playwright. Aristophanes mocked Euripides for loving Agathon long after he had left his boyhood behind him. (Remember, not everyone followed boy-love to the letter. The idea of men loving boys until they grew whiskers did not always hold true. Boys grown ''old'' could shave their chins and butts; some men just preferred other men, hairy or not; most men impregnated boys but other men adored being penetrated.) Plato says that Agathon had polished manners, wealth, wisdom and dispensed hospitality with ease and refinement.

Aristophanes, my preferred playwright, is, naturally, the father of comedy. He wrote perhaps 40 plays of which 11 remain. He was feared by all: Plato states that it was his play *The Clouds* the root of the trial that cost Socrates his life. Nearly nothing is known about him other than what he himself revealed in his works. Playwrights were obliged to be conservative because part of each play was funded by a wealthy citizen, an honor for the citizen and a caveat for the author. He was an exponent of make-love-not-war who saw his country go from its wonderful defeat of the Persians to its end at the hands of the Spartans. Along with Alcibiades and Socrates, Aristophanes is featured in Plato's *The Symposium* in which he is gently mocked, proof that he was considered, even by those he poked fun at, as affable. *The Acharnians* highlights the troubles the Athenians went through after the death of Pericles and their defeat at the hands of Sparta. *The Peace* focuses on the Peace of Nicias. *Lysistrata* tells about the plight of women trying to bring about peace in order to prevent the sacrifice of their sons during war, occasioning the world's first sex strike. When Athens lost its freedom to Sparta, Aristophanes stopped writing plays.

Marathon). He is said to have been a deeply religious person, dedicated to Zeus. As a boy he worked in a vineyard until Dionysus visited him in a dream and directed him to write plays. One of his plays supposedly divulged too much about the Eleusinian Mysteries and he was nearly stoned to death by the audience. He had to stand trial but pleaded ignorance. He got off when the judges learned of the death of his brother at Marathon and when Aeschylus showed the wounds he and a second brother had received at Marathon too, the second brother left with but a stump in place of his hand. In one of his later plays, Pericles was part of the chorus. The subjects of his plays often concerned Troy and the Persian Wars, Marathon, Salamis and Xerxes (Xerxes is accused of losing the war due to hubris; his building of the bridge over the Hellespont was a show of arrogance the gods found unacceptable). In *Seven against Thebes* he too tells about Oedipus' two sons. This time the boys agree to become kings of Thebes on alternate years. Naturally, when the time comes for them to change places the king in place refuses, which leads to both boys killing each other. *Agamemnon* is an excellent retelling of the Trojan War, as Agamemnon sails home to be murdered by his wife Clytemnestra. In *The Libation Bearers* Agamemnon's boy Orestes returns home to destroy his father's assassins, Clytemnestra and her lover Aegisthus. In *The Eumenides* (the Kindly Spirits) Orestes is chased by the Furies for having killed his mother. He takes shelter with Apollo who decides, with Athena, to try the boy before a court. The vote is a tie, but Athena, preaching the importance of reason and understanding, acquits him. She then changes the terrible Furies into sweet Eumenides.

Euripides may have written 90 plays of which 18 survive. His approach was a study of the inner lives of his personages, the predecessor, therefore, of Shakespeare. Due to his stance on certain subjects, he thought it best to leave Athens voluntarily rather than suffer an end similar to that of Socrates. An example: ''I would prefer to stand three times to confront my enemies in battle rather than bear a single child!'' He was born on the island of Salamis, of Persian-War fame; in fact he was born on the very day of the battle. His youth was spent in athletics and dance. Due to bad marriages with unfaithful wives, he withdrew to Salamis against Samos when the island attempted to become autonomous from Athens. He was elected as a magistrate during the Sicilian Expedition led by Alcibiades, and given for function the goal of finding out why the expedition had ended disastrously. Sophocles was always ready and willing to succumb to the charms of boys. Plutarch tells us that even at age 65 ''he led a handsome boy outside the city walls to have his way with him. He spread the boy's poor himation--a rectangular piece of cloth thrown over the left shoulder that drapes the body--upon the ground. To cover them both he spread his rich cloak. After Sophocles took his pleasure the boy took the cloak and left the himation for Sophocles. This misadventure was eventually known to all.'' He died at 90, some say while reciting a very long tirade from *Antigone* because he hadn't paused to take a breath (apocryphal but charming). Another version has him choking on grapes, and a final one has him dying of happiness after winning the equivalent of an Oscar at a festival. The first of his trilogy--called the Theban plays--is *Oedipus the King*. Here the baby Oedipus--in a plot that goes back to Priam and Paris at the founding of Troy--is handed over to a servant to be killed in order to prevent the accomplishment of an oracle, an oracle stating that he will kill his father and marry his mother. He does both after solving the riddle of the sphinx (which creature becomes four-footed, then two-footed and finally three-footed?). His mother, when she finds out she's been enjoying her own son, commits suicide and Oedipus blinds himself. In *Oedipus at Colonus* Oedipus dies and we learn more about his children Antigone, Polyneices and Eteocles. In *Antigone* Polyneices is accused of treason and killed. His body is thrown outside the city walls and the king forbids its burial, under pain of death. Antigone does so anyway and, faced with death, she commits suicide, followed by the king's son who was going to wed her, followed by the king's wife who couldn't face losing her precious son. (Wow!)

The father of tragedians was <u>Aeschylus</u>, of whom 7 out of perhaps 90 plays have survived. His gravestone celebrated his heroism during the victory against the Persians at Marathon and *not his plays*, proof of the extraordinary importance of Greek survival against the barbarians (sadly, he lost his brother at

In the second story Xenophon describes a tender battle scene in which a certain Episthenes, seeing that a handsome enemy boy was about to be executed, ran to Xenophon and begged for the boy's life. Xenophon approached his general, Seuthes, in charge of Episthenes, to ask if the lad's life could be spared, as Episthenes had shown himself a valiant warrior. Seuthes asked Episthenes if he would be willing to take the boy's place and be executed. Episthens stretched out his neck and told Seuthes to strike off his head if the boy so ordered. The boy came forward to save Episthenes, but dropped to his knees and begged that both their lives be spared. Episthenes rose and enfolded the lad in his arms, telling Seuthes that he would have to kill them or let them both go free. Seuthes laughed and, says Xenophon, winked at him. The story is certainly true as someone of Xenophon's value would never have recounted it otherwise.

Of the philosophers, <u>Plato</u> was the major source for this book. Plato's most famous allegory is the Allegory of the Cave. Humans there have no other reality than the shadows they see on the walls. If they looked around they could see what was casting the shadows and by doing so gain additional knowledge. If they left the cave they would discover the sun, analogous to truth. If those who saw the sun reentered the cave and told the others, they would not be believed. There are thusly different levels of reality that only the wisest are able to see. It's basically thanks to Plato and Xenophon that we know what we do about Socrates. Plato's perfect republic is ruled by the best (an aristocracy), headed by a philosopher king who guides his people through wisdom and reason. An inferior form of government, one that comes after an aristocracy, is a timocracy, ruled by the honorable. A timocracy is in the hands of a warrior class. Here, Plato has Sparta in mind. Next comes an oligarchy based on wealth, followed by a democracy, rule by just anyone and everyone. This degenerates into a tyranny, meaning a government of oppression, because of the conflict between the rich and the poor in a democracy.

As for the tragedians, we'll begin with <u>Sophocles</u>, author of 123 plays of which 7 remain, notably *Oedipus* and *Antigone*. An Athenian born to a rich family just before the Battle of Marathon, he was a firm supporter of Pericles. He fought alongside Pericles was killed by a soldier named Mithridates who struck him with a blow that felled him from his horse. Cyrus' head was cut off by Artaxerxes' eunuch, Masabates. Cyrus' mother had Mithridates captured and killed by scaphism, the ancient Persian way: The victim was stripped naked and placed between two rowboats that closed one on the other like a walnut, with only the head and arms and legs protruding. He was then feed milk and honey that caused a diarrhea that filled the interior space and attracted insects which ate and bred in the man's flesh until nothing remained but bone. Later she won Masabates, the eunuch, in a game of dice and had him flayed alive. After Cyrus' death Xenophon and his ten thousand made their way back home, the breathtaking account of which ends his *Anabasis*. Xenophon called the boys around him, the Beautiful Ones. The Athenians exiled him when he fought with the Spartans against Athens but the Spartans offered him an estate where he wrote his works. His banishment may have been revoked thanks to his son Gryllus who brilliantly fought and died for Athens. If Xenophon did return to Athens it was a meager consolation as the loss of a son is a man's worst fate.

Here are two stories related by Xenophon, which will give the reading insight into this wonderful man:

The first concerns Cyrus the Younger. Cyrus was going away on travels and the custom was that he kiss his relatives on the mouth. A certain lad, in love with Cyrus and wanting to be kissed too, told him that he was a distant member of his family. Cyrus said that he had noticed the lad because he never took his eyes off him. The boy blushed and said that he hadn't dared introduce himself. Cyrus said that as he was a relative, he too deserved a kiss, which he gave him. The boy said that as he too was going off on an adventure, and since Persians kissed during such times, he merited a second kiss. Cyrus laughed and bestowed it. The boy rode away but rapidly returned, his horse in a lather. "Is it not true," the boy asked, "that when one returns after a time one is received with a kiss?" "You weren't away long enough," laughed Cyrus. "How can you say that when being away from someone as beautiful as you, for even a second, is like a year?" Cyrus again laughed and told the boy he would soon join him and that from then on he wouldn't be absent for ever a second.

Olympic Games, and reading them to the spectators. As I've said, many people doubt that he actually went where he said he went and saw what he said he saw. But the same was true of Marco Polo who causes disbelief to this day simply because he never mentioned eating noodles in China or seeing the Great Wall or even drinking Chinese tea. But no historian, then as now, can write a book on ancient occurrences without referring to Herodotus' observations. An amusing example of recent discoveries that give credence to Herodotus is this: Herodotus wrote about a kind of giant ant, the size of a fox, living in India, in the desert, that dug up gold. This was ridiculed until the French ethnologist Peissel came upon a marmot living in today's Pakistan that burrows in the sand and has for generations brought wealth to the region by bringing up gold from its burrows. Peissel suggests that the original confusion came from the fact that the Persian word for marmot was similar to the word for mountain ant.

Xenophon, born near Athens in 430 B.C., was a historian and general. His masterpieces are *The Peloponnesian Wars* and *Anabasis.* He loved Sparta and served under Spartan generals during the Persian Wars. Like the Spartans, he believed in oligarchic rule, rule by the few, be they the most intelligent or wealthy or militarily acute. He spent a great deal of time in Persia alongside Cyrus the Younger. Cyrus the Younger was the son of Darius. Cyrus became very friendly with the Spartan Lysander, convinced that Lysander was the only honest man he'd ever met. Lysander helped the Spartans win the Peloponnesus Wars by siding with them. When Darius became ill, Cyrus, astonishingly, turned over his governorship to Lysander, while he went to his father's bedside in Susa. But his brother Artaxerxes, not Cyrus, was named king and Cyrus tried to assassinate him. He failed although he was pardoned, always a mistake from ancient times up to those of the Renaissance. Instead of thanking Artaxerxes for sparing his life, Cyrus the Younger raised an army, among whom were Xenophon's 10,000 and other mercenaries (all of which is the subject of *Anabasis*). Cyrus the Younger met his brother in combat where Cyrus was killed. Cyrus' mother foamed at the mouth at losing her favorite son. According to Plutarch the boy struggle of virtue versus vice. A small jest, he went on, often reveals more than battles during which thousands die. His writings on Sparta are nearly all we possess concerning that extraordinary city-state. His major biographies are the *Life of Alexander* and the *Life of Julius Caesar*. Amusingly, Plutarch wrote a scathing review of Herodotus' work in which he stated that the great historian was fanatically biased in favor of the Greeks who could do, according to Herodotus, no wrong.

Thucydides was an Athenian general and historian, contemporary with the events he described. What he wrote was based on what actually happened; there was no extrapolating; no divine intervention on the part of the gods as was the case with Plutarch. An example of this was his observation that birds and animals that ate plague victims died as a result, leading him to conclude that the disease had a natural rather than supernatural cause. His description of the plague has never been equaled, the plague that he himself caught while participating in the Peloponnesian War. He is thought to have died in 411 B.C., the date at which his writing suddenly stops. He admired Pericles and democracy but not the radical form found in Athens.

Herodotus was also contemporary to the events that interest us here. Cicero called him the Father of History, while Plutarch wrote that he was the Father of Lies. His masterpiece is *The Histories*, considered a chef-d'oeuvre, a work that the gods have preserved intact right up to our own day, a divine intervention that would not have surprised a believer like Herodotus (it's also a book I reread every year). Part of his work may have been derived from other sources (what historian's isn't?) and the facts rearranged in an effort to give them dramatic force and please an audience. Much of what he did was based on oral histories, many of which themselves were based on early folk tales, highly suspect, naturally, in all their details. Aristophanes made fun of segments of his work and Thucydides called Herodotus a storyteller. Surprisingly little is known about his own life. For example, he writes lovingly about Samos, leading some to believe that he may have spent his youth there. Born near Ionia, he wrote in that dialect, learning it perhaps on Samos. He was his own best publicist, taking his works to festivals and games, such as the my thoughts, the ruler of my actions, the aim and finality of my pleasure and felicity. To God and to you I will dedicate my heart.''

Speaking in this way, the passionate lover multiplied his embraces, ever enjoying the adorable child. He continued to delight the boy, so much so that when Alcibiades no longer had the cock in his ass he forgot what bliss meant, and begged for the return of his perfect master.

So ends the translation of *Alcibiade fanciullo a scula.*

SOURCES

(1) See my book *TROY.*
(2) See my book *Greek Homosexuality.*
(3) See my book *Renaissance Homosexuality.*

The major sources that provided the groundwork for the preparation of the translation:

Plutarch was born near Delphi around 46 A.D. to a wealthy family. He was married, and a letter to his wife even exists to this day. He had sons, the exact number unknown. He studied mathematics and philosophy in Athens and was known to have visited most of the major Greek sites mentioned in this book, as well as Rome. He personally knew Emperors Trajan and Hadrian, and became a Roman citizen. He was a high priest at Delphi and his duty consisted of interpreting the auguries of the Pythoness (no mean task). He wrote the *Lives of the Emperors* but alas only two of the lesser emperors survive. Another verily monumental work was *Parallel Lives of Greeks and Romans* of which twenty-three exist. His interest was the destinies of his subjects, how they made their way through the meanders of life. I too have a passionate interest in how men strive their wholes lives for success, only to be crushed, like Alcibiades, like Pericles, at the end. In explanation of his oeuvre Plutarch wrote that what interested him was not history but lives, and the Jekyll/Hyde fertilize the brain, but only the spunk of someone noble and distinguished can bring a maximum of benefits.''

Hearing this, the lustful boy smiled charmingly, wishing to prove through his acts that which his breathless master desired. ''Yearning for knowledge has tipped the scales in your favor, more than any other reason. I'm now ready to satisfy you.''

That said, he raised his chiton and took the pose appropriate for the situation. The master lent him a hand and his boyish cock immediately rose and lengthened, a glorious treasure that made Heaven and the stars blush with shame. The sun itself, vanquished by the celestial splendor, could only retire behind a veil.

How can I detail the incredible marvel, one of the universe's glories? The two hemispheres, celestial globes, colored by hot blood, trembling when grazed by the hand, reddening like a thousand rubies on a surface as white as milk. All was a charming prairie, a floral garden, a rainbow of scintillating stars. The cheeks' movements, regular, grave, amorous, as one would expect from a child so glorious, would have given an erection to a statue of bronze or marble. What a majestic beauty was this button of tight and delicate folds, equal to the bud of a rose, a flower of a thousand colors, purple in a landscape of snow. Before such supreme marvels the master, delirious with joy, fell to the knees of the child and his tongue, stroke deaf with emotion, entered the mouth that his lips covered, and then, avid, errant, it descended to the desired secret places he embraced, as avid as a baby at his wet-nurse's breast, licking, sucking, and, raising the legs, he plunged into the source of the delicious ambrosia liquor. Overwhelmed by ecstasy, he gave voice to his happiness: ''If Paradise is the site where souls delight in celestial felicity, you will be the Paradise of all Athens, in whom men will find their delight. A Paradise that will make men's souls happy and men's bodies too. What is Heaven's glory compared to yours? Heaven frightens men with its lightening, whereas you invite them, attract them through the promise of your gifts. Lightening reduces all to ashes, you promise life and fecundity. Your movements, as uniform as the sky, are productive, Heaven's are boring and useless. Your in-and-outs, at times slow, at times rapid, give tranquil joy and supreme voluptuousness. From here on in you will be the center of

"What also facilitates the act for the child is that he has nothing to do but feel the sensations. It is the lover who works and sweats, and this is only the beginning of their pleasures."

"Please give me a look into the others," requested Alcibiades.

"I will do so happily," said the master. "God is great and gives us all we could desire, all that is good and beautiful, without ever drying up the least source. And the lover who does everything in his power to do good and to render service, who helps the unhappy and extracts from Hell poor souls he transports to Paradise, approaches God as closely as humans are allowed. And who does this better than he who consoles his belovèd, and sacrifices all for him?

"Why do you think your ancestors, wisest of all men, placed at the top of the godhead Venus and Cupid? Because these two offered the ultimate in pleasures. And those who imitated them are now stars in Heaven, known to us as Castor and Polydeuces and Ganymede and so many others that it would be impossible to count them. Read the Greek legends and you will see the truth of what I say."

"It is indeed true because I have read them. But why are Venus and Cupid the most hallowed of all other gods?"

"Because they're the most beautiful and courteous of all the others," answered Philotime.

"Tell me again dear master," added Alcibiades, "how one can, in this way, become spiritual and savant."

"The human brain," began Philotime, "is the heart of the soul and the site of eternal intelligence, but its nature is cold and humid, to such an extent that if nothing heats it up it becomes dense, incapable of knowledge, full of ignoble secretions. It becomes animated only when stimulated by certain incitements, the topmost of which is the sperm of a wise and educated man, a miraculous substance that has this as one of its virtues: entering the body through the narrow door of the garden, aided by the boy's natural heat, it rises to the very center of the brain where it is assimilated into the soul that it stimulates. A child who wishes to equal his master has but this way of doing so. I accord you that the sperm of just anyone, as long as it is warm and temperate, can

''Alcibiades, my treasure,'' answered the master, ''perfection is found in harmony. A kiss is agreeable, but not when one bites. Scratching can please, but too much draws blood. These ruffians are not lovers, but werewolves, unworthy to taste at what is most supreme. They are murderers, enemies of Nature and the world.

''Its against the likes of these that nations make laws that punish them with death, and not against discreet lovers. What is the purpose of these laws? That one must not be the cause of hatred and disorder but the agent of goodness and love. The laws are not against doing it, but against abuses.

''As to why some children have more pleasure than others, it is because part of their garden is linked to their bird by subtle nerves, of a sort that the thrilling voluptuousness of the bird is accompanied by the pleasure felt in the garden. Some boys have such great pleasure by being ridden that they become crazy with desire and they beg, they *beseech* their lovers to mount them. These children are keener and more ardent than others because the abundance of lascivious spirits that inhabit them are greater, and make them agile and hot for action, to such an extent that they move sensually at the hips and provoke lascivious in-and-out thrusts. Some boys are calmer and do not yell out their desire but they don't give themselves any less to caresses, desirous of doing it like the others. I can tell you, without fear of being disavowed, that there is no child who can resist such pleasures. I know some even so avid, so greedy that they can stand no pause, no interruption when serviced by a cock. They caress it, ram it in themselves with the lustfulness of goats, to such an extent that I wonder if they didn't experience it already while in the belly of their mothers.''

''How is this possible?''

''The cunt of a woman is like a virile member inversed, towards the end of which the child directs his hole so that he can take his part in conjugal pleasure. He becomes so used to it that, later, it is for him a cruel torture to not be scratched there.

''Women know this pleasure too, and many abandon the use of the fig for the other, and take their delight like boys.

that upon which our life is based and which involves the most diverse qualities of the body, finds its sources in fondling those parts that are the softest, the best and noblest made. That's why lips avidly encounter lips, those perfect purple roses in the midst of a face as white as milk. Our agile hands, audacious, make their way to our nipples and our ass cheeks, because therein there are no bones, no obstacles to the satisfaction of our desires. We push onwards, not only onwards but deeper, for it is there the real object of our desire, there where, as all philosophers and savants admit, is the center of our nerves: in a word, the height of voluptuousness is the genitals, which are masses of nerves, both subtle and delicate. It is there the supreme center of sensuality, and when awakened, like the violin's bow awakens music, they are aroused as they are created to be. And to speak frankly, that pleasure would not be complete without the emission of semen, which is in itself the concentration of all that is life itself, which, being liquid, can transmit, from these organs of pleasure, the secret of life, all the while giving us divine orgasm. Small boys are not of an age to have this seed, which means that they have little interest in the active part of lovemaking. But they have a tickle of voluptuousness, the harbinger of real, later, joys. Nonetheless their nerves are subtle enough to provide stimulation, to move them, which is why a boy's bird rises at every occasion. Incapable of doing it to others, they concentrate with extreme violence on themselves and on their garden where they receive enjoyment, the reason why they so love to be caressed, fondled and entered. Their intimate parts are bathed in the warm spurts of sperm that stream over them, giving the boys an incomparable carnal enjoyment and feeling of fulfillment in having so visibly satisfied his lover, as the warm substance runs into every crevasse. The sensuality is wondrous and overpowering. But this pleasure depends in a huge part on the experience and deftness of the lover, because one finds, in the world, true brutes, and the tears, cries, blood and spasms of the tender and the innocent are for them dastardly trophies.''

''But why don't these men procure pleasure, since the same causes have the same effects?''

"On this important point, my heart, I wish to answer with facts. It is difficult for me to believe, my dearest, that you yourself are a novice in this matter. I'm sure your supreme grace and your exquisite gentleness have drawn to you the eyes of numerous lovers. A flower as precious as you can only allure desire to pluck it. There have certainly been other bees, active and industrious, who have sought to imbibe your honey. It is impossible that your incomparable charms have been, until this day, unsolicited. Do not pretty boys in their cribs and at the breasts of their wet-nurses receive lascivious caresses from enflamed lovers? And even breezes that envelop them with love, do they not do so in light cuddling, ready to kiss, embrace and take their pleasure? If it is such with children, what must it be for you in the spring of your full bloom?"

"I won't deny," answered Alcibiades, "that numerous lovers have, to this day, followed and sought my favors ardently and with implacable tenacity. But the equally implacable barriers raised by my parents have given no possible entry for the realization of their desires. I have had some exchanges with boys my age who did for me what I did for them, but the pleasure seemed in no way what you describe with men. There is certainly as big a different between these first attempts at pleasure and those of which you speak, as there are between green fruit and that which is ripe. That's why I may be willing to give you a chance, and why I listen so keenly to what you have to say."

"Then let's get down to it, my son, as reality will teach you much better the truth than even the best discourses," said the master in full erection.

"Such is my desire," said Alcibiades, "but I fear that once you have what you want you will become somber and lose interest in any form if discourse. So please, continue with your explanations."

"And so I shall," said Philotime, and went on: "The pleasure received by boys under men is not the same for all. Our senses have an object, and when well regulated the resultant sensations are highly agreeable. In such a way do we appreciate beautiful painting; music that pleases the ears, perfumes the nose, delicate food our tongue, but the most perfect sense, the most admirable, boys act, how insolent, loud and lewd, I suddenly become calm because I also see their angelic grace. At the view of their stimulating apples of Paradise peace enters my heart and my soul, and I am agitated by the combined need to be both severe and loving, an agreeable and healthy equilibrium.

''We can't express that love to all school children because of their age and reputation and social standing, but we do our best to avoid being accused of partiality and injustices, in order to harm no one. We show marks of benevolence to all, but there are degrees and proportions, and to he who is preferred we show no special favors, and those favors that are shown are done so in secret, and are the pleasures of Adonis. We love all our boys and respect them equally. Each feels himself loved and honored, and so it is that the master satisfies all, while satisfying himself.

''The master who does not love *in secret* is an ignorant ass, and his school a prison and he the jailor. Did not Jupiter hide himself in the form of a bull in order to pursue love? Did not Hercules disguise himself as a woman in order to possess his belovèd? And is it not normal that he who prepares the land has the right to harvest its fruits? You offer me a wondrous cave of wines, and you would want me to die of thirst? Would it be right for just anyone to come for these boys? That just anyone could harvest the fruit, deflower all, and only the gardener would not have the right to his pleasure, taken with reserve and with discretion?''

''You plead your cause very well,'' said Alcibiades, ''but allow me another question. Tell me, sincerely, what pleasure we boys get out of all this if we lend ourselves to your caprices? Personally, I can't see one. We are only placing ourselves in a humiliating position while undergoing your assaults, as one is sacrificed, hung high, butchered, tortured on the wheel, disemboweled and quartered. If you seek your pleasure in the misfortune of others, you cut yourself off from the justice of men and the laws of Nature, those that forbid you to harm those around you, and especially helpless children. For boys who have experience in such things, it's their fault. He who knows what is demanded of him and accords it must not complain.''

the boy that it is the boy himself who will do the inviting, so hungry has he become to play the game of love. "

"How does one go about it?"

"The boy, on the bed, must stretch out before the eyes of his lover, his cheeks raised and the passage into his garden always central. The boy keeps his bird half in and half out, as it were, giving himself pleasure by rubbing his stomach against the sheet while the part out stimulates the ardor of the lover, the view of which is the first of the joys of love. And if the boy plays with himself or his lover takes his bird in hand, so much the better.

"What is of most importance is that in this way one can please all boys, no matter what the age, even the youngest, and one can multiply the pleasures. The lover will not devour the boy's bird like a starved wolf, but will suck on it, and lick it ever so gently."

"But," interrupted Alcibiades, "fathers do not want teachers to use children in this way, and those who do so lose their reputations and are dishonored."

"These fathers are right because the severity that one employs in education cannot be reconciled with caresses and amorous voluptuousness. These parents also respect the laws and ordnances enacted against boy-love.

"But judicious masters know how to reconcile severity and gentleness. They know that one without the other are both useless and dangerous. And that severity alone makes of the master a barbarian and the student his slave.

"Indulgence and kindness alone will make the boy insolent and ill-mannered, refusing to give his master the slightest respect or submit to his authority. But combine both and you work miracles. Love does not preclude obedience. Giving pleasure voluntarily is not treason. A child honored by caresses does not expose himself to shame and contempt. In fact, he becomes an object of love for his class and for his master. Those who do not profit from such a wondrous occasion do a disservice to themselves.

"The character of a child--indomitable, proud and unreasonable--is such that if uncorrected by love these bad instincts could lead to grievous mistakes. When I see how badly of a good time with your wife when she's accompanied by her parents, cousins and visitors, plus questions of contracts and dowry?''

''Before going further with me, my master, please satisfy my curiosity on other points. If one doesn't wish to go with women or boys, can one not assuage his ardors by himself with his own hands, without spending money, without fatigue, without submitting to anyone? Thanks to this means, we have immediate and infallible remedy for each and every sensual itch.''

''Alcibiades my belovèd, jerking yourself with your own hands (*se pomper les humeurs avec ses propres mains*) is a miserable expedient which deprives us of our true being and kills our passion for the real thing. It's not only our semen that comes out, it's our very blood. It alters our features, makes us pale, and can even hasten death. Nature puts everything in the preparation of our dew, for it is that which regenerates our species. She makes it with the purest part of our blood, an enterprise that weakens our veins and saps the vital parts of our bodies. If we satisfy ourselves with our hands it becomes a habit thanks to the ease of doing so. Whereas pleasure we have with the person we love calms our spirit and contents our desire. Jerking leaves us unfulfilled and tires us out because, due to its facility, we do it so often.''

''What is the best age, dear master, for pleasure with a boy?''

''From 9 to 18, but it depends. Some boys retain their freshness late, others fade early, and there are even infants that give you a hard-on when in their cribs,'' (*qui vous font bander dès le berceau*).

''But how can one so young be large enough to satisfy desires?''

''That's complex. Some are just naturally elastic enough, others become so through the habile efforts of their lovers. The secret is patience. Lovers must never impale their belovèds as do the barbarians, up to the hilt, reducing boys meant for joy and voluptuousness to blood and tears. A good lover knows how to discreetly amuse his boy until he feels no pain, and by doing so the lover will increase the intensity of his own orgasm and make himself deeply desired by his boy, who takes more and more pleasure in the game of love. That is the key: to be so wanted by is her game. And even the lowest of them, dirty and as dumb as a cow, who sleeps on straw and converses with beasts, who couldn't distinguish the cock of a man from that of a donkey, would marry the simplest peasant were he to show her the slightest interest.

"And if she couldn't even find that, she would oblige her noble master to find her a city dweller, one with a dowry! And if not, she would go to court and accuse her master of having her, she a virgin who had fallen into the wrong arms, to whom she had afterwards been faithful, when in truth her dirty wide-open cunt had welcomed the cook and his helpers, valets, whoever and whatever would ride her.

"Just try to imagine the arrogance of girls of good birth, if whores believe their cunts are so inestimable. So really, do you think for a moment that a boy of breeding should become mixed up with such animals? I could give you a hundred reasons why you should stay clear of them, and there are men of great talent who have written volumes on women, but even then, what was written was far below the reality. Could one of value exist? I won't deny it but it would be a miracle! As for me, I haven't, in my whole life, met a single man who has found a good one.

"Another point. Because rapports with women cannot be kept secret as they can with men, one risks being treated as a miserable fornicator. A woman wants all of a man, and even then she is unsatisfied. A mistress is always behind you, spying everywhere. Old women you know are for her your pimps; your friends? still more pimps; young women? your mistresses; boys? your sluts. You must cut off contacts with everyone and cloister yourself with her. And even the occasional pleasure one gets with her becomes insupportable because of the ulcers, pus and discharges due to her menstruating."

"Get married," advised Alcibiades, "and you will find a remedy for all these inconveniences, and you will find yourself in an ocean of voluptuousness."

"Poor Alcibiades. Always the same food without the slightest variety. To lose the finest part of one's soul, one's freedom, inestimable treasures, and for what? To find easy pleasure and common delight, a feast where even flies are invited! And so let's say that one marries, what then? Do you think you'll have much voluptuous garden, there is nothing either disgusting or smelly. To the contrary! It reinforces and spices one's desire.

"Those who like melons must not be put off by either their taste or scent. All worldly things, to be perfect, must maintain their attributes. Bread and wine have their unique savor, just like the ass of a beautiful boy has its particular aroma and its perfume of amber.

"One day a wise man, while licking the hole of his belovèd, became aware that he had perfumed it with rosewater. He withdrew his tongue, interrupting its work. How is it, he asked, that I've come to please myself with your flower, with its natural musk, and you've filled your ass with the whole boutique of a perfumer!

"In the midst of a thousand boys you will not find one with a major fault. That said, a judicious boy-lover will not choose injudiciously among boys. To have veritable pleasure he must not go with the first boy who presents himself, just because he has an ass and a hole. What are apples among some are not necessarily among others, and instead of a garden one is offered infected latrines. A suitable boy must be noble, well brought up, clean, well groomed, neat, affable, without stain. Only then is he an inestimable pearl.

"Where one finds impurities men must use all their arts to clean and purify. Here we can compare boys with fruit. When they are good they are exquisite. When rotten, they are detestable and foul.

"But even should a young lad, inexperienced and penniless, show some signs of uncleanliness, even then it is nothing in comparison to a woman's repugnant menstrual infliction."

"Tell me dear master," said Alcibiades, "how is it that women make such hoopla of their fig, and show themselves vain and indiscreet?"

"It comes from the fact that she wants a despotic and absolute power over men. When she can, she shows herself arrogant and cruel. Our money, goods, freedom, reputation, our lives even, are nothing in comparison to her assets. She pushes her lovers to cut each other's throats, their gushing blood a trophy to her glory. Fires, ruins and the devastation of cities and kingdoms

"As for a woman's liquid that you've qualified as stinky, what would you say if, from the same place, issued juice that we find in boys, his shit? Do you think it smells like ambrosia? Do you find the odor of musk in manure? Would the entry to Paradise, for you, be a chamber pot? Are these objections imagined or serious? Am I dreaming or telling the truth? What says my venerated master?"

"Your divine intelligence, Alcibiades, is worthy of you. But one can find arguments that are both alluring and well founded. I'll refute them one by one. The difference in pleasure in having a boy's bird in one's hand and a woman's breasts, is as great as having something full of life and something inanimate. The breast has neither movement nor sentiment. The bird is mobile, vivacious and graceful. Breasts are inert and without a soul. The bird stirs, thrashes about and is frisky, it shakes its head, cries and smiles and takes an active part in sensual combat. Breasts are full of air, empty, often flabby, more often disgusting than exciting.

"And doesn't a young boy have nipples, small, it's true, but as such more handsome and precious in the same way a rose in the form of a bud is more beautiful than when fully open. A woman's garden is far more restricted than a boy's because a woman holds back her fruit, does not open her ass, and seeks pleasure in but one place, her cunt. That is why the taste of a woman is bitter. Whereas a boy is always ready to give pleasure, begging for it even, and his whole body is ready to give and receive bliss.

"And as for the liquids that float around the cunt, and its dimensions, an abyss as large and deep as the ocean, I'm convinced that after giving her cherry, to the day she gives birth, no boy is capable of penetrating to the bottom of her chasm.

"And when you speak of the slight stain supposed found in boys, it is not true! A boy well born and well raised shows never a sign of being soiled. To the contrary! His is a natural perfume that embalms his hole, as can be seen when the glans exists, its head exposed, naked, proud and triumphant from the battle of love, dripping with essences and suave perfumes of Arabia. And even if there were the slightest odor, the smallest visible trace from his cushions, lightly covered in down, conceived for the concavity of our lower abdomen, the rounded cheeks coinciding with our pubis, is it not the height of felicity? And when one mounts a boy, one is bereaved neither of his kisses nor by the joy of his breath, perfumed by his amorous mouth. There too the union is complete, the intoxication shared. And the man can turn and take his belovèd face to face, his member in his garden, or gently play against the boy, according to his caprice. And when you take the lad's bird in your hands, feel it become inflamed, stand proud, stretch out fully, is that not the ultimate pleasure that inflames you, that invites you to attack harder, to multiply the strokes, to plunge deeper, fired by love?''

''But,'' asked Alcibiades, ''the form that a boy's bird takes, is it of importance to the pleasure between the lover and the belovèd?''

''Of course it must be well proportioned, neither too small nor too gross. Too small does not excite desire. Too big in only good when one reverses the roles. For me I like the member hard, rising from two small round stones, which will distill into my hands the wondrous dew. The bird is an instrument that gives and takes pleasure, nothing is more precious--as is yours, my belovèd.''

While speaking Philotime had one arm around the boy's shoulder, while the other explored the depths of his secret parts.

''Then tell me master, do not women have apples like boys, ready to offer themselves to the bird for which you have such high esteem?

''For me,'' continued Alcibiades, ''the apples I prefer are those in front, which fill so precisely the hand. If it's apples you search in love, women have four, while boys just two. If a boy's garden has fruit, that of a woman too, which is even more precious, more desirable. If in boys you have the peach, in girls you have the fig, as tasty as any other fruit. As for the cunt that I've heard compared to an inextricable labyrinth, it is a criticism too general to be true. Such vastness is found only in those who use it often or are overly ripe or have had children. But for the young, it is a baseless calumny.

his neighbor be also, in turn, repaid? Why must a boy be called disgusting if he receives money for giving pleasure?''

''No, beautiful enfant,'' began the master, ''a mercantile arrangement is one thing, the exchange of favors something else completely. There is no rich and powerful man who doesn't need, at some time, someone smaller than he is, for which payment is the right of he who offers a service. I think it is entirely acceptable that a generous lover comes to the aid of the child he loves and who pleases him on every occasion. That aid can be bountiful but devoid of self-interest on both parts.

''On these occasions love must be the unique rule, love alone is the only judge of what is honorable in delicate questions. Love permits presents, benevolent proofs of love, generosity, but never sordid venality.

''Priests who live honorably earn far more from their altars than priestly mercenaries. Why? Because they are venerated, while the others are despised.

''Authors of comedies, whatever their talent, are vilified if they demand payment, the reason why, in ancient Rome, they were deprived of a tomb.''

''I'm completely satisfied with what you say, but now tell me please, if one has more pleasure with boys than with women, and why.''

''Some find that the ultimate in erotic satisfaction is with women, that Nature has gifted them with secret, soft, warm parts that, when entered by the virile male member, facilitate coitus, enliven voluptuousness. And the voluptuousness, this quivering of two bodies, two epidermises, aided by ardent kissing, an act during which one loses oneself in another, in desire, is the only way to find true fulfillment. It is the essence of love. The tongues interlace, suck, breathe in the images of the other, the object of one's love. Both souls inhale into the heart, each in turn, the breath of Paradise. Both bodies intertwine, like indissoluble vines. Both bodies form but one soul. Nothing is missing in their desire. The mystery of love is completed; nothing is lacking in the interminable orgasm.

''But a boy's flower, my dear Alcibiades, does it not enclose the very same Paradise? And even more, those two rounded not permit the nobility of your doubts to be troubled by prejudices and by ridiculous beliefs.''

''Could you tell me why,'' requested Alcibiades, ''boys who give pleasure to men are dishonored with injurious epitaphs like queer? (The French word is *bardache*, meaning a passive homosexual.) Why does one despise them? Why are they considered infamous? If what you say is true, isn't what is said, that they are nothing more than queers, in opposition to the reality of things? Please help me understand.''

''The word queer,'' answered the master, ''must not be given to such boys who, through affection and courtesy, give of themselves graciously to honest men who deserve their favors. In the same way one calls whores those beauties who, to satisfy the need for love, kindly offer themselves to poor suffering hearts. It is therefore reasonable and just that discreet, wise men replace these odious names by those of gods for the first and goddesses for the second. The first should be called redeemers of human misery, the second the consolation of the weak and in distress. Moreover, many great princes have raised altars and temples, consecrated by priests, to them, with offerings of incense and with sacrifices. Many such stories come to us from ancient Greece and Rome.

''But there exist rent-boys who work only for money and who love only money, as there are veritable priests and those guilty of simony. They're both covered with the same dignity, they both administer the same sacraments, but one does so in excellence, and his character is sublime and he shows only interest is the spiritual needs of his flock, a man contented with the accomplishment of divine laws. The other seeks monetary gain. The result is that the first is sacred, the second detestable. Those things without price should never have a rate fixed to them. And what is more precious, more worthy of boys in love, noble and divine Alcibiades, than to give to men, without ulterior motives of benefit? The boy who gives himself for money is vile and infamous, and instead of being the gardener and treasurer of fulfillment in love, he is the ignoble destroyer of his own flesh.''

''Isn't it reasonable,'' asked Alcibiades, ''that he who renders services to others be remunerated in return? That he who helps

47

the laws of Nature. In forbidding commerce with foreign children, he allowed commerce with one's own.

''From the laws of men, based on caprice, we pass to those of Nature, which are universal and infallible. These are more in favor of the love of boys than against, which I shall now prove to you.

''We call laws of Nature those accepted by each man, sect, every nation, and that from the crib. These laws are sanctioned by the wisest and most just. They are divided into two parts. The first is our homage to God, the other is our goodness to our neighbor.

''*Always love God and love your neighbor as you love yourself*, or which is the same: Do not offend either God or neighbor. These are different and must not be confounded. There's no rapport between either. So I ask you, if your neighbor is happy with what you desire, if he's content, touched, can one then say he's been offended? Have you transgressed the principle of love your neighbor? Have you shown offense? Will he haul you to court?''

''No,'' said Alcibiades, ''your neighbor will be obliged that you have not offended him. He will even owe you a favor. The difference between such action and an offense is like that between a gift and a theft.''

''Perfectly put,'' intervened the master. ''And in the same way, if a child consents to give himself for the pleasure of his lover, if he finds joy and advantages, where is the offense? Wouldn't it be mad to try to find one? If our free will, that wondrous gift of God, gives us the will and the power to dispose of, as we wish, what is ours, why would we make an exception of giving one's body? You can loan a house, a horse, a dog, but you can't loan yourself! Is there a master so cruel as to free a slave and then forbid him to profit from his freedom? God made us free in order to then make us slaves to our passions!?!

''How can God, who has made us fragile, blame us for our fragility? It would be blaming His creation. Could He be pained by our happiness, or jealous of our pleasures and delights? If our enjoyment didn't give some consolation to our poor lives, we would be just as well in Hell. Man would not be the king of animals, but the sum of the world's torments and suffering. Do

46

temperature, that dries and burns the earth. Its atmosphere is both thick and inflammable.

"So when the legislator passed by the lake with his army, the ignorant soldiers interrogated him concerning the strange properties of the waters, their color, heat and the rest. This was the perfect occasion for the legislator to gain the support needed to arrive at his ends.

"Now, his army was composed of some women whom the long march had not only made ugly, but also undesirable to the point that they could enflame the heart of no man. So the men among the troops reverted to their usual practice, the easiest and most natural for them, and turned to one another, leaving the women out in the cold. The commander of the troops was quick to see the long-term effects of the men's reticence to honor women, the disappearance of future replacements, meaning he would soon have rule over no one. So he ordered the boys to no longer have commerce among themselves, adding that it was God's will. The proof was that God had engulfed, in celestial anger, five villages that had practiced such mores before being inundated by the lake of sulfur. In this way did the legislator deprive the boys of the wondrous pleasures they had shared among themselves.

"So you see on what are built laws! Meanwhile the legislator and his descendants, perfect hypocrites, built, next to their temples, houses dedicated to boy-love. By appealing to Heaven these men are considered devout, all the while reserving for themselves the sweet privileges of access to boys. Legislators, as well as the best-known writers, under the duplicity of virtue, justice and severity, preferred, for themselves, life to the truth. Convincing in this way, violence becomes unnecessary. One can appeal to the good nature of peoples, their kindness and their generosity, things annihilated by violence. Where there is no violence there is love and peace. A violent man is a tyrant, in opposition to God who wishes accord between souls.

"Another legislator, a truly great man, had nothing bad to say against the love of boys, and moreover forbad men from deserting their children for the children of foreigners, and that those who sought out and helped native children were deserving and virtuous, whereas those who favored foreign children violated

45

legislators who pass their erroneous legislation, mixing it, at every instance, with the sacred and the profane.

"Nothing shakes our reason more than the atrocity of the tortures we are threatened with should we persevere with our form of love. We all have the respect of God engraved in the depths of our hearts and our eternal soul. He is the essence of all. He controls our very existence and how long we will exist, and so deserves our respect and adoration. That's why He is everywhere the object of our cult and our fears. It's on that basis that legislators founded their rules. They say that it is God's wish-- and certainly not their own caprice--that their decrees be given prompt application. They instill in us a sense of complete horror in even thinking of disobedience, something they dilute in the milk we imbibe as babies in the crib. It was in such a way, with such artifices and subterfuges, that Lycurgus and Solon and other famous legislators forced through their laws and assured their powers.

"And especially by adroitly including God in their plans they were able to control a huge population, torn apart by revolts and factions. And, prudently, they brought in natural phenomena to concord with their decrees. They thusly take control of the population, simple folk of little education, ready to obey, having been nursed to do so."

"But if God is as all-seeing and immutable, as wise and clement as one says, why has He not intervened in condemning the pleasure that is for some a crime?"

"A clock owes its movement to the wheels and the counterweights built into it by the clockmaker; in giving the time it fulfills its function. In the same way our own workings are what God and Nature installed. To abandon them is to distance oneself from the very aim, the very reason of our creation.

"Now let us tackle certain traditions that have had a hold over us. Around Arabia and Syria, due to the combination of certain elements or perhaps those unknown, we find an immense lake of bitumen that gives off an odor of gas. It renders services, for health and for the arts. It cures multiple illnesses and is vital in the construction of vessels, and a plethora of other works. Its viscosity renders it inapt for navigation, as well as its extreme and eat and fuck like beasts. Tartars have laws that permit them to screw their mothers, sisters, sons and brothers. Laws that permit intercourse among males are upheld by some of the most civilized of nations, the Persians, the Medes, Indians and the most noble of Greek cities.

''Do you find it just, Alcibiades, that ridiculous laws are enacted everywhere, by peoples like the Chaldeans whose god is superstitious, inconstant, cruel and lacking in judgment?''

''No,'' replied Alcibiades, ''all this is crazy and highly unreasonable.''

''But they endure,'' insisted the master, ''sanctified through usage and time, reaffirmed through the fears they themselves inspire, held to be true and legitimate and, because of the gullibility of the simple-minded and the severity of governments, they live on and stand for justice itself.

''But let's return to the heart of our subject and review these gods in whom we have complete confidence. Is not Jupiter the king of gods, and did he not make off with Ganymede? But we are not gods, so where Jupiter used force to fulfill his needs, we must rely on prayers. And didn't Apollo find full pleasure with Hyacinth, and Heracles with Hylus? And if Cupid himself is our own sex, if he is a boy, is it not proof that our sex is superior? The love of women is represented by Venus, who has neither quiver nor arrows, unless lent to her by her son Cupid.

''So it is that boys possess of the coveted scepter, while women possess something far inferior. Those who believe the gods do not hold the scepter as the supreme sources of voluptuousness, and that those who taste of it deserve punishment, are as far from truth and justice as a slave who is punished for executing the orders of his master. If you believe such nonsense then you might as well followed those illiterate souls who think that at night the sun hides in a hole somewhere on the moon.

Those who, in their own private interests, believe it appropriate to forbid such voluptuousness, knowing that such a defense would be found irrational to men of good sense, seek to uphold such laws by invoking the immutable power of God. And like hypocrites who use sermons to help pass their lies, so do complimentary to himself his existence would be imperfect. There would be no one to ease his ardor. He would lose his genius, become inactive, miserable, the worst off of all animals."

"Give up our plans to seduce children," said Alcibiades, "and your torments will come to an end."

"We have no power to renounce love, my dearest Alcibiades, and even less to abandon love for the wondrous object that enters our hearts by our eyes, and is drawn to the soul of him whom one contemplates. We cannot cease dreaming of the infinite bliss of possessing he who is contemplated. We cannot cease dreaming of the infinite joy of possessing him, he who excites our desire, who inflames our love. And he who is not intoxicated by the pleasure so wished for, who is not submerged in its opulence, who does not dive into its depths, is consumed by fire until reduced to ashes. What counts is to drink the liquor that impregnates our lips with its sweetness, to drink of his substance is what counts, whether the vase be round or square means nothing.

"The laws of certain people, in particular those of the Athenians, as you say, forbid this form of love. Men bend the laws to fit their interests, but their interests are not always just. These laws were created to come to the aid of the weaker sex, that which is incapable of its own protection, born to be subjugated. It was in their favor that the law prohibiting congress between males was formulated, a law in the interest of the State and politics, not one founded on reason and the natural penchant of Nature. Execrable laws of this kind, based on human and religious chimera, are welcomed by pious, stupid, sacrosanct rednecks.

"Silly people who make silly laws can be found everywhere. One people, the Vanges, have invented an infallible god, the creator of the universe, that lives only among them, and has no more power than their own chief, who is himself considered a god. Beyond their borders there is no other god, no other truth. They push their presumption so far as to claim to be the only chosen of God. Their hubris knows no limits, pretending even to be superior to God, and that it is He who obeys them, and in their theaters they poke fun at God, making him a comic buffoon.

"Scythes hate the faith of their enemies so much that they massacre them all, and swear only by their gods who have mouths

''Alcibiades, my love, what an infant you are! Tell me. If you were to invite a prince or a pauper to your table, would you conduct yourself the same way with both? Certainly not, and now you want beasts treated the same way as men? With the same honors at your banquet? Between men and beasts there is an inequality of nature, of senses, of condition, and you think there is no inequality in acts! And if beasts were in competition with men, why not have them compete also against houses or cities or the arts? So if Nature, who is supremely intelligent and always goes straight to the plan she has in mind, without ever deviating her route, if she gave man, her most beautiful creation, such noble attributes, then she couldn't refuse him that other place of pleasure, which she owed to him and to herself as the creator. She has beasts eating the same food, whereas for men she has created a confusion of variety. The same is true of amorous sensations. And if a man receives a noble person at his home, can you imagine him offering something common and vulgar, while he has so much in abundance?

''In nature one rooster will demand of another his tribute in love. Partridge males fight one with the other for the same conquest, the loser giving himself to the winner so he can satisfy his lust. Dogs, the closest animals to men in intelligence, render each other the same service, as does the lion, when his mate is bearing, turn to young male lions for play. And dolphins, unhappy with their spouses, turn their love towards the children of men. One, in love with the beautiful singer Arion, came to his assistance when thrown overboard by his mates, and carried him to shore. Another, in love with a handsome schoolboy, took him from his school to his house, and from his house to his school, a distance of two miles. And on the island of Rhodes a dolphin cared for a boy, taking him wherever he desired, obeying his every caprice, in perfect harmony. The boy, in thanks, gave himself discreetly to the desires of the animal, reaching heights of ardor that the waves encouraged by their movements. To gain virtue and ease sorrow, men must climb one on the other, sufficing unto themselves as God too relies only on himself.

''If men couldn't find in boys mutual help they would be unhappy and pine away. If a man couldn't find in a boy someone this not the case because it renders so many, many services? Do you mean to tell me that we should limit it to one purpose, while at the same time limiting that other part of the body to just one usage, the most vile, the most disgusting of all? That part of us that can offer so much enjoyment, can provide so much happiness, a part that is so perfect, so noble, that Heaven in its honor made it spherical?

''No, no, Nature has reserved a seasoning that adds savor and charm to the ass. If the cunt serves as a passage for both urine and pleasure, why cannot the other also serve for sensuality among its prerogatives, why limit it to the latrines?

''Nature, if she so limited things, would be sterile, jealous of happiness, improvident and tightfisted in offering pleasure. But the opposite it true. Nature in all her glory does her best for us, especially for our enjoyment!

''To not use these gifts would be outrageous, it would be putting oneself outside Nature, it would be revolt against Nature, and as such one would merit being crossed out of the book of life. If she gave us pleasure it's for our delight. And we can render her homage and celebrate her as being most dear to us, honoring her foresight, the wealth of her inventiveness, making her the most wondrous of mothers.''

''If this is true, of what use are women?''

''My dear Alcibiades, man is guided by his instincts, the first of which is to reproduce himself so that he will continue on, from generation to generation. For this alone, women must not be abandoned, nor enslaved, nor frustrated in the love that we owe them. We make children and at the same time we take our pleasure, and women achieve their greatest dignity. It is true that some men prefer women to boys, but Nature produced this affinity to ensure the survival of the species; others who shun boy-love are simply vulgar ninnies. And then, a boy's flower wilts rapidly, while that of a woman lasts far longer, happily for her. But it's because a boy's spring is so short that we give ourselves completely, and frequently and intensely in the love of boys.''

''If this is the case, dear master, why then do we not find such penchants among animals, where Nature reigns even more supreme than with us?''

me from such doubts, master, or renounce putting me through such terrors.''

''My adorable child, those who talk about what is against Nature are part of the nobility. They know that what is rare is valuable, so they want to make access to the flower rare, the pleasure of which is fit for only them. That is its unique object, blissful contentment. It's in recognition of pleasurable enjoyment that Sparta made laws binding boys to men. The man will appreciate a boy's garden until the flower has passed its time. The man will then seek a new flower and the boy, now a man, will seek a flower of his own.

''My duty is to open your intelligence to the truth, to give you, gradually, an overview of all things. So let us take your arguments one by one. You say it's against Nature, but as said, that is the ignoble argument used by nobles. Here is the source of the mistake. A woman's cunt is placed opposite the flower, the anus, and the use of the flower is called against Nature only because man is born through the cunt, which is natural. But this is a misnomer because whatever is derived from Nature is in itself *natural*, and laws dictated by Nature itself cannot be *unnatural*. That's the proof. An act is natural when Nature drives us to accomplish it, when she makes us desire it.

''So if one has a natural penchant for beautiful boys, how can that be against Nature since Nature herself draws us to that penchant? Nature never ever does anything in vain. There is nothing useless in Nature. If she creates beautiful children whose beauty draws us to them, do you think she would leave us stranded, unable to fulfill our desires? Don't these beauties exist for a reason? And since she always brings accomplishment to what she creates, would she leave these beauties beyond our reach? Useless? No, no, these are charming objects made to satisfy desire, the only aim of which is pleasure.

''And does not Nature accomplish this among those who are the most sensitive--artists, philosophers and teachers? And is there not a greater resemblance between men and boys than between men and women? In giving boys the loving traits of girls, Nature encourages us to find pleasure among both. Is one's hand not considered the most estimable and precious among organs? Is you, my kisses, my caresses, the permission to fondle my boyhood, but never will I allow you to go beyond that!''

Alcibiades left Philotime who gained courage with a plan to succeed later on. For the moment he took himself in hand, giving himself pleasure, all the while with the image of his adored angel before him, discharging into his fingers. (*Il se déchargea sur ses doigts du soin de le soulager, et ne cessa de se représenter à l'imagination, pendant la jouissance, l'image do son ange adoré.*)

Despite everything, Philotime was determined to achieve his goal. Nothing other than his need to have the boy submit docilely to his desires motivated him. He therefore decided, on another occasion, to open himself up the lad. ''A reasonable person, dear Alcibiades, must achieve what he reasonably desires. What is the cause of your obstinacy to accord me what I wish, why resist the ardors of your loving master, so in love? I know that you refused my advances, the last time, by forwarding arguments that I find lack maturity and reflection. I wish to know more of the reasons for your cruel refusal, which will eventually lead to my death, because should I not succeed, I will sacrifice myself rather than offend you. I'll accept without resistance the mortal blow from your gaze, that you use against me like so many daggers, and I shall quietly die.''

''My wish is not to cause you suffering, my dear master. Were that the case, I would be indeed cruel, ungrateful and unjust. There are other reasons, clearly pressing and, I believe, invincible. And I will reveal to you one: What you propose is clearly a horrible vice, one revolting to Nature, known to all as a vice against Nature. Our laws prohibit it. Athena, the founder of Athens, found it despicable. I've heard it said that the gods themselves struck against cities dirtied by it, rained down fire and floods to burn and submerge them. And for that reason we find today, on such lands, sulfur, from which grow trees whose fruit, when opened, contains ashes and coal, traces, dear master, of the vengeance of the gods. And punishment doesn't end there, for the souls of the damned, separated from their bodies, go through horrible, eternal tortures. You certainly don't want me to go through all this due to a vice that I find repugnant, appalling and scares me? Do you not fear such horrendous perils? Either free beginning of class, to do certain important tasks that required, in order to be well done, more time. The child, ever willing, arrived early, ending his master's impatient wait, hours during which he could not act, when he ran from the balcony to the door and back, each time he heard footsteps. ''What's keeping him! He's deliberately making me wait, playing me for a fool!'' He thought the time had passed, long before it had come! And then suddenly the boy was there, and his life began anew.

When Alcibiades arrived, Philotime took him into his room and as usual covered him with kisses, which Alcibiades was by now accustomed to. The master introduced his hand into the lad's hidden places, those destined for love and concupiscence. Philotime panted and his hand trembled while foundling him. When the lad saw his master's cannon rise, ready for action and entry into his flower, his young eyes filled with tears of pain (*quand it vit son canon affûté prêt à batter la place, et à entrer par la brèche…*).

''How can you envisage something so shameful?'' he asked, backing off. ''How can a person of your standing dishonor a boy of good family? If a man of your age and stature commits such things, then there are no limits to the crimes youths such as I, whose blood is far hotter, can commit. Do you do this to other children? And if so, what do their parents think?''

Alcibiades said the words with displeasure but with enough respect for Philotime not to flee.

''Alcibiades, my beloved son, someone who loves you so deeply as I, does not merit your hatred. When Eros pierces a heart, age and the difference in sexes cease to exist. Your divine image has entered my soul and reigns there as an absolute sovereign. Love burns in my heart since the day I laid eyes on you. If you refuse to open your garden to me you will become an assassin, a parricide, for I love you like a father, with all the force of my soul, and I shall kill myself if not fulfilled. Don't repudiate me as a lover, for my standing as a teacher is equal to your royal blood. I bow low before you, awaiting your sentence of life or death.''

''Dear master, I don't wish to dishonor you. Temper your desires, be discreet, take what I give you and will continue to give coveted. So he decided to await the propitious moment, to bide his time, never punishing the child for his errors, always offering him sumptuous gifts and compliments. And the boy, happy to be treated in such a way, smiled and showed himself to be grateful. Profiting from his contentment, one day the master waited for him in a passage, kissed him and pressed himself hard against the young body. As agile as a falcon, faster than lightening, his hand slipped inside the chiton to discover the secret parts that they avidly explored.

The boy made to turn away in disdainful wrath, but it was this kind of provocative resistance that quickened the man's desire and spiced his natural lust. He insisted and Alcibiades let him caress the delicate fruit in front and the voluptuousness of the wondrous, celestial twin apples behind, his finger, shaking, finding home in the garden paradise, and the ecstasy of his desire, as yet unfulfilled, he could easily conceive thanks to the contact of the sweet entry, the marvelous felicity to be his. This pleasure, this charming prelude, lasted until he was pulled away by urgent business. He was nonetheless intoxicated by the awakening of all his senses, and the blessed consolation of what he would eventually possess.

He was away several days but felt the ethereal serenity of a mere mortal who had quenched his partial thirst at the source of heavenly mystery, he but a man, leaving only the completion of the veritable act. We've already said that Philotime knew the art of pleasing to the highest degree, and in fact there had never been a boy, all naturally heathen, who had not succumbed to his affable and courteous ways, sooner or later, throwing himself into his master's arms. Not one who didn't finally accord him what he desired. Not one who was not worn down by his affection.

In the same way that the beauty of Alcibiades surpassed that of all others, Philotime knew that the pleasure to be his would also be far superior. That's why the impassioned tutor trembled with desire, and felt an invincible and pressing ardor to harvest the flower that Love offered him. The lad's complicity, the depth of his passion, and Love itself pushed him towards the commission of the sweet act of violence. So the next day he encouraged Alcibiades to come to school an hour before the accustomed master's wounds with a kiss that gave life and death, that transfixed the poor man's heart.

''That was not a kiss one gives a loyal friend, but one offered to an enemy. To a friend one gives his tongue, which penetrates the mouth. The mouth is its true home. Please, let me fill you inside. Yes! Like that! Like that!'' Thusly assaulted, the boy backed away and became pale and shaky. Philotime reassured him: ''Have no fear, my son, the tongue in the mouth can do no harm. The knowledge you seek in coming to me will be obtained when your tongue and mine are one! The eloquence you wish to learn from me, that your teachers sought in vain to teach but that my devotion will bestow on you, you will only obtain when your tongue nuzzles my own.'' And holding the boy against his breast, he punctuated each word with more kisses.

Philotime gave full pleasure to his desire, his very soul on his lips, his entire life concentrated in each embrace. To describe the movements that agitated the man are beyond my intelligence and language. My pen fails at its work, leaving only my thoughts free to explore the mysteries. And my jealously, fired by the scene, awakens in me disquieting desires, giving free rein to my imagination, visions of what went on to the contentment of the tutor.

But this was not the accomplishment of all his wishes. His passion was not limited to kisses. The kisses were but the harbingers of love, trumpets announcing the glorious act that was the aim of his devotion. Kisses were nonetheless full of painful bitterness, like a starving man after a long fast who is permitted only a brief taste from a table laden with food, forbidden to satiate himself. The master died at the thought that he would be limited in such a way, and he concentrated all his forces on his efforts to succeed, leaving aside all else as void of interest. It was this venture that filled the thoughts of his days and the dreams of his nights. The endeavor, he knew, would be arduous, the attempts perilous, the execution potentially filled with scandal and shame.

His soul, fired by the charms and graces of the beautiful boy, was distressed as if in the depths of Hell. He knew there would be no rest, nothing to moderate the ardor of his desire, nothing to cool the embers, except the fulfillment of the pleasure he so

When this new Cupid, the angel of Paradise, had been placed by his tutors into the ready hands of his master, Philotime gently took him aside, and after examining him with enthusiasm and avidity, spoke to him thus:

"By your royal aspect and divine grace, gentle boy, my soul is moved by unusual feelings of humility and adoration, born from my ardent desire to content you. And should you wish as much, our mutual understanding would do miracles in combining my experience with your capacity to learn. I count on the openness of your character that will allow me to be even more affectionate with you than your father, and enter into your mind a dew so fertile and agreeable that it will seem supernatural. I won't use rough methods in instructing you, as is usual, but ways that you will find congenial. And so to begin with, let me offer you an affectionate kiss." Docilely, the boy lent himself to the man's embrace.

No iris had colors so fresh, no prairie in April had flowers so alive as those under the lips of Philotime as he caressed the proffered cheeks. And as children shirk severity in favor of sweetness, so too did Alcibiades find pleasure in opening the treasures of his affections to his teacher. Suddenly the fears that accompany boys when they enter school vanished, replaced by confidence. Alcibiades found in his master's devotion the zeal to be assiduous in his schoolwork in order to please him. The only singularity between Alcibiades and his schoolmates was that the classes would take place in semi-seclusion, in private, in a separate room.

All of this was part and parcel of the master's plan. The firebrand shot from the hand of all-powerful Cupid that pierced his heart, inflamed him with an incomprehensible violence, a devastation so complete that the only move left to him was to find an access into the boy's hidden garden--or die. "Blows, hard knocks, my handsome friend, are how other masters teach," said he to the boy. "But I prefer, in their place, love kisses, in honor of your distinction. So receive this mark of tenderness, my son, and do not soil your royal soul with ingratitude, and kiss me once more." Always forthcoming, the boy opened and closed his

His nose, a gracious curb above his mouth, a true marvel for the eyes, a symbol of other, hidden, treasons, was itself a wonder, but not less so than the nostrils, symmetrical and voluptuous, fine and delicate, as white as milk, a shadow above the upper lip, another sign of his supreme beauty. His neck compared favorably with the other parts of his body, neither too long nor too short, adorned by veins of blood, hot and quick, an admirable base for the superhuman allure of his face.

His hands were promising in comparison with the rest, slender and graceful, the fingers already capable of the voluptuous gift of love, soon to grow stronger and more virile, capable of waging war.

As for the other members of the body, alas covered by jealous veils forming a barrier to covetous eyes, seemed nevertheless an invitation to one's desire to raise them and contemplate the secret places where one could take one's pleasure in other ways than in thought. There was a wondrous symmetry between what was seen and what was hidden.

Yet the inestimable jewel of his treasures was his angelic voice, each word pronounced with harmony, each pause musical, like that of a Siren, softly intoxicating the soul, not to put it to sleep but to awaken it to the torments of love.

When he opened his celestial mouth, those in audience were stupefied, thrilled to the point of ecstasy, giving way to their souls through their open lips, souls that flew to encounter the soul that was his. The human voice has the gift of taming wild beasts and enlivening even stones, as we know from the fables of Orpheus and Amphion.

That angel's tongue was the lightening that stunned hearts, a chain that in the prison of love seized the souls they held captive. His laughter, modest and charming, was a treasure of joys, a messenger of love in a garden of marvels. He was grace personified, an immortal gift of God, a gift that one cannot explain through words, one that speaks only to the heart, that attracts as if by magic, that captivates and purifies through celestial and divine beauty, that strips one of what is only terrestrial and human.

foresight, he knew the secret of conciliating hearts, of inseminating solid and profound knowledge into the natural intelligence of others, proof he was worthy of his veritable vocation.

Noble Athenians were jealous of those who succeeded in placing into his worthy hands their deeply loved sons, the very best of themselves, entrusted to a man reputed as a true refuge against the harms that threaten the young, a man whose reputation was beyond reproach. Moreover, there was no learned youngster who had not drawn their instruction from the well of knowledge that was this great teacher.

Alcibiades was thusly entrusted into his able hands and, with assurances that the boy would be respected, the master was given full power over his charge. In comparison to the beauty of this new entry, the other boys lost their radiance in the way that the coming of the dawn extinguishes the brilliance of the stars, Eos eclipsed by Helios. Diane in her woods, among her nymphs, had less brilliance and less allure and less grace than did Alcibiades taking his place alongside his master.

In the supple, gracious way he carried himself, in his easy, harmonious movements, one could see he was made to open hearts and control souls. The beauty of his curls, deployed like flowers, fell to his shoulders in ringlets. His eyes, shadowed by the veil of his lashes, were an azure-bleu with nuances of ivory, and were wonderfully proportioned and noble, shooting more arrows of love into the hearts of those who gazed upon them than the images of the objects they reflected. His forehead, majestic, was as pure and serene as a spring morn. His cheeks radiated the hue of roses melded with the white of lilies on an oval surface that surpassed the delicate Gardens of Tempe. The coral of his divine lips embellished their reddish tint and even insensitive statues would have found new life in their embrace. Oriental pearls in Doric alignment shone through his angelic mouth, delicately brushed by his violet, slender tongue, an invitation, not for bees to make their honey, but for the heavenly gods to collect ambrosia for their divine banquets. How the stars blushed in comparison to their radiance!

ends thusly:

"But your bestiality, Timarchus, is known to one and all. For just as we recognize the athlete, even without visiting the gymnasia, by looking at his bodily vigor, even so we recognize the prostitute, even without being present at his act, by his shamelessness, his effrontery, and his habits."

Aeschines finishes by reminding the Assembly that when they return home their young sons will ask them how the case the decided. "Does the Assembly want to tell them that it is now permitted for a boy to defile his body with the sins of a woman (being used as a woman)? Punish this one man. Do not wait until you have a multitude to punish."

Timarchus was indeed found guilty. He left his trial and hanged himself.

ALCIBIADES THE SCHOOLBOY
By Antonio Rocco
Translated from the French by Michael Hone
1630

Alcibiades was of the age when Nature plays the charming game of gifting bodies of divine origin indecisive traits, so that the loving eye that lovingly purveys them fails to distinguish between the sexes. He had the youthful air of the beautiful Ganymede that Jupiter descended to mighty Troy to steal for his heavenly bed, where he became a god in human forms. The most charming of ages was that of Alcibiades, an inextinguishable treasure of voluptuous promise, in which each and every one could find what he held most delightful in love. The boy offered a double perspective, fulfilling the wish of those who sought out young girls, and those, wiser and more savant, devoted to handsome youths.

Such was our Alcibiades when his tutors, in their inspired insight, judged him apt to attend school. The most fortunate of mortals was Philotime, selected among many to be his master. Having reached the age of his upmost virility, worthy in aspect and carriage, Philotime had achieved a point of equilibrium between good sense and the senses. Prudent and gifted with but against the man who let him out for hire and the man who hired him. Moreover, the law frees a son, when he has become a man, from all obligation to support or to furnish a home to a father by whom he has been hired out for prostitution.

''As soon as the young man has been registered in the list of citizens, and knows the laws of the state, and is able to distinguish between right and wrong, he is responsible for his acts. If he then prostitutes himself, which is a reckless sin against his own body, and then seeks to address the Assembly or Senate, he shall be put to death.

''Now, a certain Misgolas got Timarchus into his own home and because Timarchus was well developed, young, lewd and in the very bloom of youth, Misgolas did what he wanted to do and Timarchus wanted to have done.'' Aeschines gives no detailed information as to what the sexual acts consisted of so as not to shame himself or the Assembly. Yet he gave a list of men who were shining, pious examples of how men should behave. Three of these men were Themistocles and Aristides who were fighting for the same boy, the outcome of which was Aristides' expulsion from Athens, while Solon wrote this:

Blessed is the man sweaty from the gym,
Having muscles, supple, strong and slim,
Goes home where he may drink wine and play,
With a fair boy on his chest all day.

Meaning that Aeschines was in no way speaking against male-male sexual couplings, but was referring exclusively to the law against a rent-boy later serving and addressing free Athenian citizens. He then goes on about Homer: ''I will speak first of Homer, whom we rank among the oldest and wisest of the poets. Although he speaks in many places of Patroclus and Achilles, he hides their love and avoids giving a name to their friendship, thinking that the exceeding greatness of their affection is manifest to his hearers who are educated men. His lament following the death of Patrocles is proof of his love for him.''

Aeschines goes on about beautiful boys who hadn't stooped to prostitution, going so far as to give a list of their names. The trial

An Athenian could do, sexually, as he wished with a slave, a foreigner and a metic. He could have sex with another Athenian, but he could not sell himself unless willing to give up all civil rights. If he became a rent-boy he could no longer appear before any assembly and plead or ask for aid for any reason. If he ever hid his having sold himself and then appeared before an assembly and was caught at it, he would be stoned.

Aeschines' father was a schoolteacher and Aeschines, born in Athens, tried teaching before distinguishing himself in the army, and finally becoming a government official. As such he went to conclude a treaty between Athens and Philip of Macedon. He was accused of selling himself to Philip by a certain Timarchus, an accusation of treason that Timarchus brought before the Assembly, the penalty for which was death. Aeschines struck back by bringing a counter-suit against Timarchus claiming that he had no right to speak before the Assembly as he had sold himself on the waterfront of the Piraeus when a boy. Timarchus was thusly forced to stand trial, giving us the first and only full account of male sexual relations in ancient Athens.

Aeschines began his speech by stating that Timarchus knew he had no right to appeal to the Assembly because ''he knows that we live in a democracy, which means we live under the rule of law. Thanks to these laws a teacher cannot open a schoolroom or the gymnastic trainer the wrestling school before sunrise, and the law commands them to close the doors before sunset, for the law is suspicious of men being alone with a boy, or in the dark with him. No person who is older than the boys shall be permitted to enter a changing room while they are there. If anyone enters in violation of this prohibition, he shall be punished with death. The superintendents of the gymnasia shall under no conditions allow anyone who has reached the age of manhood to be alone with the boys. A teacher who permits this and fails to keep such a person out of the gymnasium will be liable to the penalties prescribed for the seduction of freeborn youths--death.

''If any boy is let out for hire as a prostitute, whether it be by father or brother or uncle or guardian, or by anyone else who has control of him, prosecution is not to be against the boy himself, arrows hit their marks. Dead, Alcibiades was decapitated and his head bagged for Pharnabazus. His companion for a night, younger and faster, managed to escape.

But Plutarch maintains that Alcibiades had been killed by the brothers of a girl whom Alcibiades had seduced, and so his death had nothing to do with either Lysander or Pharnabazus. Both Nepos and Plutarch agree on what followed: Another friend, a whore, Timandra, found the headless body that she wrapped in his Spartan cloak and had cast into the blaze, a pyre less worthy than that built for Achilles, Patroclus and Hector (1).

Exactly like the Sparta he loved and admired, Alcibiades is one of the strangest, most original, most enigmatic creatures to have adorned the Earth. Lustful, intelligent and beautiful, even in boyhood his admirers had made him aware of every erogenous zone on his body, far in advance of the friends his age. He knew human nature and weaknesses thanks to his enlightened guardian Pericles, whose home and bed were replenished with girls offered him by his whore mistress, Aspasia, and whose salon was graced by the greatest philosophers and dramaturges the world has known. Just as importantly he allowed his body to serve, valiantly in battle, erotically in sex. Charm, class, a come-hither regard that could stagger, an orator capable of enthralling an assembly, a manliness that inspired other men, a self-confidence that won over diamond-in-the-rough Spartans and cynically jaded Orientals. People were truly fond of him, they genuinely liked to be around him, and so exquisite did he know himself to be that when Socrates chose *not* to lie with him, he honestly admired the philosopher's unfathomable restraint before such perfection. In the whole world I can only think of the Florentine Lorenzo *Il Magnifico* who comes close, although without Alcibiades' beauty and military expertise.

[The full life of Alcibiades can be found in my book *Alcibiades*.]

SEX IN THE TIME OF ALCIBIADES: ANCIENT GREECE
As seen through the Trial of Aeschines against Timarchus
346 B.C.

drinking them under the table and screwing among what Thracians considered their nobility, as well as among the dregs. But as there is no honor among thieves, as soon as the Thracian brigands learned that the Athenians and the Spartans were set on Alcibiades' death, they began to plunder his wealth, daring him to do anything about it. He fled into the interior of Thrace but as the robbery of his possessions continued, he finally sailed back to Persia, to the satrap Pharnabazus. Bewitched by Alcibiades, now forty, who had lost none of his charm and little of his beauty, and who had known kings, princes, and generals, Pharnabazus offered him not only shelter but also the revenues from the town of Grynium. Believing he could do better, Alcibiades decided to see the great king himself, Artaxerxes II at Susa. He also knew of Lysander's contacts with Cyrus the Younger, and the attempts of both men to replace Artaxerxes with Cyrus. He felt he could advise Artaxerxes on how to avoid being overthrown by his younger brother, and how to avoid mounting problems with Sparta. Perhaps fearing that Alcibiades would enthrall Artaxerxes as he did Pharnabazus himself, Pharnabazus refused to help Alcibiades in his quest to travel to Susa. The Athenian left anyway. Lysander learned of his departure and informed Pharnabazus that if Alcibiades were not handed over alive or dead, Sparta would end all collaboration with Persia. Lysander, in turn, was being pressured by the oligarchy he had set up in Athens, men whose survival depended, they felt, on eliminating Alcibiades as a future menace to their very survival.

Alcibiades put in at a town along the way to Susa and, wanting company for the night, Cornelius Nepos tells us, took a young Arcadian, a loyal friend, to bed. Pharnabazus' men had followed him and very silently heaped brush around the habitation, which they then set on fire. Awoken by the light and crackling of the blaze, and guessing at its origin, Alcibiades flung his Spartan-style cloak around his left arm and took up his sword in his right hand. He and his friend threw as much clothing as possible on the blaze, making a narrow passage threw the flames. They leaped through a window and, naked, confronted men who immediately backed away. But they were outnumbered, and even from a distance many of their enemies' numerous spears and outnumbered the Spartans in ships and tried to engage them in the Hellespont, in view of Alcibiades' fortification. The Athenians anchored in the harbor of Aegospotami, the Spartans at Lampsacus. Soon a daily routine set in. Day after day the Athenians would sail from Aegospotami to Lampsacus, but the Spartans always refused to leave their protective harbor to fight. The Athenians would then sail back to Aegospotami where they would disembark for a leisurely meal on the shore and horse around as boys and men are like to do at the beach. One day Alcibiades left his lair and came down to warn the leaders that they should be more on the lookout, and the army far more disciplined. The Athenians gazed on Alcibiades, atop his horse, his purple robe open to the navel, his skin oiled, his hair and beard carefully curled, and shook their heads in wonder at this man who had lorded it over Athens since his childhood, and who was now in self exile. Some knew him, some knew him even very well. For them all, this was just Alcibiades being Alcibiades. They thanked him because it was conceivable he would live to reign again over them all. He rode away, his long robe spread over the horse's ass.

When the Spartans felt that the time was ripe, they set sail for Aegospotami where they attacked the Athenian forces, asleep in the shade of the afternoon sun. There was no battle. The men on shore scurried into the hinterland and those on the ships surrendered. Of the 180 vessels present, only 20 got away. Four thousand boys and men, then and there, had their throats cut, depriving them of their lust and their beauty and their already much-to-short lives.

Alcibiades, who had been deified a few short months before by the Athenians, was now, after the defeat, vilified for his arrogance and general depravity. The people knew about his castle on the Hellespont and hated him for it, wondering why such a fortification had been deemed necessary and how much of Athens' treasury its walls protected. The castle was located in Thrace, a land known for its barbarians. There, Alcibiades had his own private army which he used to despoil his neighbors. Cornelius Nepos tells us that, as in all the other countries Alcibiades had lived, in Thrace too he had seduced the local louts, rhetoric and natural gifts." Luckily, a little later Alcibiades' superheroes found themselves in difficulty during another battle, and were saved by the rabble soldiers they had thumbed their noses at. The result was that they all kissed and made up, and had a huge barbeque during which bread and meat were thrown around, from one man to another, as a sign of friendship.

As general, Alcibiades led his ships into the Hellespont to gather money and sailors. He went from victory to victory, doing wonders for Athenian morale. Soon Alcibiades was Athens' uncontested leader. Before he personally returned to his homeland he sent his troops into the city to tell of his glorious victories, thereby assuring his triumphal arrival. Only then did he bring captured Spartan galleys into the Piraeus, loaded with spoils, bedecked with dancers, lyre players and drummers, his own ship rigged with his signature purple sails--the indisputable hero of his people. He made his way to the Acropolis through throngs of delirious well-wishers. Cornelius Nepos goes on to tell us that he gave a speech in which he blamed the Fates for his troubles, and not the Athenians, now shedding tears, who had nonetheless sentenced him to death. (The hypocrisy was, of course, mindboggling, but as usual he knew exactly what he was doing.) He emphasized the fact that he had influence over Tissaphernes who promised, Alcibiades assured them, to make sure that Athens and Athenians never lacked for food or money, even if it meant that he, Tissapernes, "ended up selling his own bed." He was applauded, his estates were returned, and priests annulled the curses aimed at him. From here on the Athenians went from victory to victory until the entire Hellespont was theirs. Alcibiades was given complete charge over the war and carte blanche in any attempt to come to terms with Persia. But victory is an unfaithful mistress.

Alcibiades returned to Samos and tried to engage the Spartans, but they were too wary of his power. They bided their time until he went off to the Hellespont to gather money and additional soldiers. The Spartan navy chose that moment to strike and win a series of battles. Alcibiades lost the backing of Athens, and rather than lose his life too, he retreated to a castle in Thrace that he had had the forethought to construct. The Athenians still

Back in Athens the women went on the world's first sex strike, hoping to force the men to make peace before making love. But Greece being Greece (at that time, at least), this was hardly a hardship. There's an anecdote that comes down to us through a play by Aristophanes, *Lysistrata*. One of the women in the play, who had taken part in the sex strike, now complained about how impossible it was to get sex once a woman was old: "It's the same with men," a man answers. ''Not at all,'' the woman continues. ''Any grey-haired man can pick up a young girl, but a woman's season is short.'' (She didn't foresee the advent of cougars.)

It was at this moment that Alcibiades chose to reenter the scene. He sent negotiators to Samos to inform the Athenians stationed there with their fleet that he could arrange an alliance with Tissaphernes who was at the moment in favor of the Spartans. But Tissaphernes wanted an end to Athenian democracy, favoring an oligarchy headed by Alcibiades--whom Tissaphernes trusted--instead. The Athenian population on the island, believing themselves every bit as qualified to represent Athenians as were the Athenians in Athens, decided to forgive Alcibiades--with, perhaps, the ulterior motive that he would still be able to bring Tissaphernes over to their side, a sentiment that Alcibiades encouraged. The Athenian general Thrasybulus, stationed at Samos, was sent to bring Alcibiades to Samos where he was made general. The island was known for its beautiful boys, one of whom was sought out by all generals and politicians passing by. He was Bathylle and the poet Anacreon had his portrait painted, giving these instructions to the artist: ''And between his charming, incendiary thighs, paint a noble member that aspires to be loved.''

The men on Samos adored Alcibiades as he had been adored wherever he set foot. Right off the bat he won a series of victories so grand that the soldiers and sailors felt exalted and glorified. And Plutarch goes on: ''The army directly under him felt so superior to the other soldiers that they wouldn't mix with them.'' He added that, ''While others had known defeat, Alcibiades' men were invincible.'' Although Thrasybulus was responsible for many victories, ''it was always Alcibiades,'' says Cornelius Nepos, ''not Thrasybulus, who reaped the glory, thanks to his golden

But again Nicias changed his mind. This too was sad because historians believe that had they set off immediately, Nicias and his men would have been able to make their way, on foot, to Sicilian colonies that were still in their corner. But Syracusan spies infiltrated Nicias' ranks, telling the soldiers that the roads leading away from the harbor were blocked, and that they would do well to prepare themselves before confronting the enemy. This they believed and remained a day too long, the time needed for the Syracusans to really block the passages out. The Athenians had thusly to fight their way through the enemy, which caused damage in the ranks, but the worst destruction was reserved for laggards, consisting of the weak, the wounded and the sick. As usual on the battlefield, dysentery was a mortal enemy, emptying the body of its substance in the most despicable fashion known to men.

Nicias finally sued for peace, offering to pay the stupendous sum of a talent per man spared, a sum that would be guaranteed by Athens, putting the city-state in debt for years to come. The Syracusans refused, and the Athenians continued their death march. Hungry and dying of thirst, they made their way to the river Assinaros, one that would have a dreaded reputation for all time to come. Here the Athenians literally climbed over each other to gain access to the stream, while Syracusans, catching up with them on horseback, slaughtered them with arrows and spears from the banks, but even then the men drank water muddy and red with blood. The survivors were rounded up and sold into slavery, most of whom were sent to stone quarries where they disappeared from history. The lucky ones, those who were handsome, were handed over as sexual slaves, and there is at least a chance that they were well treated. Nicias, whom the Syracusans held responsible for the misery and death of so many Sicilian warriors, was tortured in the most miserable fashion, says Thucydides without going into detail, before his throat was slit. The Syracusans had been forced to fight for their survival, and as such must certainly not be blamed for wanting to keep their freedom. So content were they that from then on, each and every year, they organized festivities in honor of their victory, festivities known as the Assinarian Games.

real reason for Alcibiades' treason was the hope that the Athenians would, in desperation, recall him.

And this was a possibility as things were going very wrong for Athens. Inaction on the part of Nicias and his advisors gave the Sicilians time to build more ships and rearm. They were not accomplished sailors, far less so than the Athenians, but they were fighting for their lives and survival as a people, an incredibly strong incentive. During a first naval battle at Plemmyrion, a harbor very chose to Syracuse, the Athenians fought in a restricted space unfit for their large vessels but perfect for Syracuse's smaller ships. Reinforcements promised by Athens arrived late, held up by storms, after the Syracusans had inflicted great damage. Athenian land forces then tried to capture a Syracusan fort atop a cliff overlooking the harbor. When this failed, the attackers tried to withdraw, which caused panic among those still climbing upwards. Men lost their footing and attempted to cling to what they could after flinging away their spears and shields. Most fell to their deaths, a reported 2,000 in all.

Nicias met with his advisers who all counseled withdrawal back to Greece. But Nicias, perhaps fearful of the consequences when he confronted the citizens of Athens, perhaps suffering from the Trojan complex--he and his men called women as the Trojans had been when they lost their city--decided to carry on. Alas, no one had the authority to stop him. He did decide, however, to abandon the Plemmyrion harbor. But before he could, an external event made him change his mind, which is sad because had he done so, he would have escaped with his life and ships. But Nicias was a superstitious man who believed in signs and omens. One such sign was a full eclipse of the moon, an omen that seemed to indicate that he should remain where he was. This gave the Syracusans time to block the entrance of the harbor with every ship and floating vessel at their disposal, all linked by heavy chains. On the hills surrounding the harbor local villagers turned out to watch from an incomparable bird's-eye view. Over the days that followed they saw one side win the battle, only to be undone the next day; the Athenians on board the ships cried victory one moment, while moaning their defeat the next. In the end the Athenians abandoned their ships in favor of an escape overland.

wool. At no time would skin come into contact with skin. Alcibiades would have ejaculated in this way, into the fabric. The boy too would have ejaculated thanks to the pushing of his penis against the tissue and rocky surface, or he would have brought himself off with his own hand, hidden in the folds of his own cloak. In this way historians have attempted to bring understanding to the multiple texts on the subject, each vague and contradictory, about how men had sex with young boys they called striplings. As usual with wondrous Sparta, nothing was ever crystal clear.

Alcibiades had been sentenced to death when he hadn't returned to Athens, and now he was again sentenced to death, this time by the cuckolded Agis. It seems that Agis had no difficulty in believing the rumors of his wife's unfaithfulness simply because for a period of ten months that followed an earthquake--the magnitude of which had scared him out of his wits while copulating with her--he hadn't dared approach her again. Leotychides had been conceived during this time. Luckily Alcibiades was forewarned, giving him an opportunity to flee to his supreme enemy's camp: the Persian Tissaphernes.

Tissaphernes was the governor (called a satrap) of the western part of Phrygia, Lydia and Caria, a diplomat, a general and a key advisor to King Darius II. And he was right up Alcibiades' alley in the sense that he too was a lover of guile, an admirer of rogues, as well as being wonderfully subtle. He was also 40, an age during which a man especially appreciates a boy's beauty. And there was no one more beautiful and intelligent than Alcibiades, possessor of behavior so smooth it anesthetized the Persians into believing everything he said. In fact, Tissaphernes named his most beautiful garden, containing streams and meadows, pavilions and baths, Alcibiades Park, the name it was referred to ever after, a pleasure retreat both men shared during Alcibiades' sojourn. The situation was indeed remarkable as Tissaphernes loathed the Greeks for the disaster they wrought on Darius I and Xerxes. He was also, Plutarch says, psychopathic and perverse. Yet he ended up flattering Alcibiades even more than Alcibiades--an expert--flattered him. Thucydides wrote that the him, the soldiers also felt that under someone indecisive like Nicias the war could drag on for an eternity, with no riches, as Alcibiades had promised, at the end. Alcibiades agreed to return but on his own ship.

Unknown to all, his true destination was Sparta. A Spartan nurse had cared for Alcibiades and had instilled the love of Sparta in the child's heart. Also, his family had had traditional connections with Sparta. When a Spartan delegation came to Athens in search of a peace agreement in 421 Alcibiades, thanks to his family, enjoyed privileged access to the ephors. Alcibiades didn't waste time in seducing the Spartans. He wore their coarse clothes, bathed in cold water, ate their disgusting broths, drank their inferior wines, and fucked their women, one of whom was King Agis' wife who bore Alcibiades' son Leotychides. Alcibiades counted on Leotychides to found a new Spartan race of Alcibiadesian origin. It didn't help matters much when Agis' wife went around calling her baby Alcibiades, the name she preferred to Leotychides. Alcibiades could play the role of the perfect Spartan, Plutarch tells us, because he was the perfect chameleon-- all things to all men, displaying virtue or vice as the occasion called. It must have been marvelous to observe his technique because men really liked and appreciated him, and being a man's man is not an easy task. Plutarch goes on to say that in Sparta he devoted himself to athletic exercises; in opulence-loving Ionia he enjoyed the luxury of the baths, oiled and perfumed, at ease with the fondling of both sexes; in savage Thrace he drank to the dregs among the dregs; in phallocratic Thessaly he awed all with his horsemanship; and in refined Persia he exceeded even the Persians in magnificence. He was thusly accused of playing a double game, but men have been known to willfully march to more than just one tune without having treacherous motives.

Alcibiades' sex with Spartan men would have been rapid and carnal, but with a Spartan boy he would have taken advantage of a hunting expedition when, sheltered probably by a rocky outcropping, he would have lain alongside the lad, both enrobed in the traditional wine-red Spartan cloak. He would have pressed his cloth-enclosed erection against the other's buttocks, perhaps occasionally reaching around to caress the lad through the folds of vessels the expedition had seen at Segesta had only been the same vessels passed from house to house and from temple to temple!

Alcibiades wanted to be judged for the crime against Hermes before setting sail for Sicily, aware that during his absence his enemies, were he not judged now, would do what was necessary to turn heads and buy votes. After all, the penalty for heresy was death. Athenians were as serious about offending the gods as were Europeans, later, under the Inquisition. Had his request to be judged before setting sail been accepted, he would have certainly been acquitted for the simple reason that the Athenians needed him for their intervention. But the request was refused, and he prepared to leave for Sicily as co-general with Nicias at the head of what Thucydides said was the greatest armada ever raised by a single Greek state, 134 triremes and a far greater number of smaller ships, as well as 30,000 men. Diodorus Siculus recounts that all of Athens--inhabitants, friends, lovers and children-- traipsed behind the warriors as they made their way to the Piraeus, singing and waving fronds. The ships bobbing in the harbor had been fully decked out with banners, flags and pennants, their sides covered with the shields of all the participating countries, those furnishing soldiers or money. Perfume burners and fires in bronze vessels consumed incense in such quantity that the air was misty with it. Lovers kissed their friends goodbye and the boys went off to their fates

Just after arrival at the island of Sicily, a ship, the *Salaminia*, came from Athens demanding that Alcibiades return to stand trial for the destruction of the Hermes' statues. Judging from the behavior of the emissaries sent to bring him back, Alcibiades knew what awaited him at home. He knew that the Athenians had perfected the art of using men for their own benefit, but that they would then humble and chasten them when the men became too powerful or too well known. This was a highly dangerous move on the part of the Athenians because the army and sailors favored Alcibiades, who had an uncanny way of winning over the men under his command; the Athenians therefore treated him with kid gloves, promising anything to get him aboard. Otherwise, they knew, the whole army would mutiny. Besides the army's love for

The problem with Sicily began in 415 B.C.--the 17th year of the Peloponnesian war--when a delegation from the island came to tell Athenians that the time was ripe for them to conquer Syracuse, the most important city-state on Sicily. The people of Syracuse were ethnical Dorians, as were the Spartans, whereas the members of the delegation from the much smaller city-state of Segesta were ethnical Ionians, as were the Athenians. Syracuse, the island's principal city, was about the size of Athens. It was rich and the island richer. Its capture would supply Athens with immense wealth, resources and more wheat than Athens would ever need. Sicily was the breadbasket of the Greek world, as, later, Egypt would be for the Romans.

Alcibiades wanted to go to war and soon he had the Athenians on their knees, drawing sketches of the island in the sand, each vying to place the major island towns in their right places. Men and boys were forming lines to join up as members of the expedition, certain that they would reap gold through sacking the palaces and homes of the rich inhabitants. The delegation from Segesta arrived with 60 talents of silver (a talent weighed 26 kilos) and plates of solid gold. In addition, they declared that their temples and citizens possessed a treasure in solid gold vessels. The Athenians sent a delegation to assure itself that this was so; the members returned with smiles on their faces. This turned the heads of the Athenians, and especially that of the handsome Alcibiades who was always in need of lucre.

When the Athenian noble Nicias saw that Alcibiades had stirred up the blood of Athenians hungry for war and the riches reaped through war, he threw in his support, so long as he was named general and the size of the fleet and the number of warriors involved in Alcibiades' plan were at the very least doubled, thereby giving Athens a chance at success. He did warn his friends, however, to beware of Alcibiades who would one day endanger Athens in order to live a brilliant life of his own.

When the full Athenian force did finally arrive in Sicily, it discovered that the solid gold brought to Athens by the Segestaeans was only silver plated with gold, and the solid gold young age. The philosopher Bion suggests that he had indeed begun early on: ''Even as a child he made men unfaithful to their wives, and as a young man he made women unfaithful to their husbands'', just as Philotime had foreseen. Aristophanes tells us in *The Frogs*, ''They love him and hate him, but cannot do without him.'' He wrote another play, lost, entitled *The Man with Three Dicks,* in which Alcibiades' erotic exploits were satirized. Alas, we know not in what way.

Statues of Hermes, god of travelers, were erected at crossroads. Their particularity was a fully engorged phallus with ample foreskin. As crossroads were places of encounter, the phalli took on erotic signification. Boys looking for adventure would stroke them for luck, girls searching for husbands did likewise, and women wanting children made pilgrimages to the sites--in fact, the phalli were polished to a luster. During the night preceding an expedition to capture Sicily, Hermes' phalli throughout Athens were vandalized, most probably by drunken pranksters, exactly the milieu frequented--and most often led--by Alcibiades, a youth known by all for his brilliant intellect and total absence of morality. As during our own times, in ancient Athens too people were unduly respectful of those of high birth and affluence, the reason they were reluctant to attack Alcibiades head-on. The destruction was also heresy, as Hermes was an Olympian god. And it was the worst possible omen prior to a military enterprise. But there was a strong possibility that Alcibiades would escape punishment thanks to his connection with Pericles and his immense wealth.

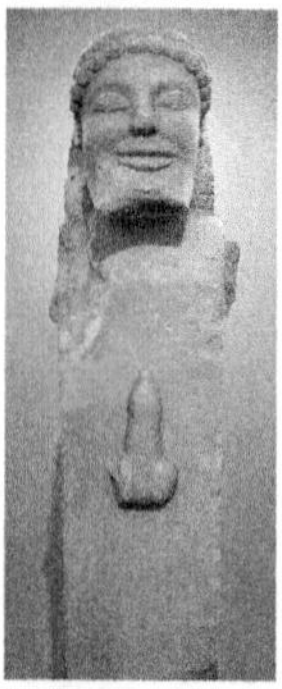

Hermes statues at crossroads

what they wanted from ''nice'' boys, there were always whorehouses. They flourished throughout Athens. The ones for boys had courts where the lads sunned themselves, naked, their wares in varying states of arousal. But whorehouses offered compensations. With ''nice'' boys, men often had to content themselves with intercrural sex, performed upright with the penis inserted between the thighs, while in whorehouses they could penetrate anally to their hearts' content. They could also get blown, otherwise a seemingly rarer occurrence in antiquity than anal sex.

Cruising areas were the market place, back streets, in the martial arts schools, in cemeteries, along the quays of the Piraeus and in the Ciramicus, the potters' quarter, northwest of the Acropolis. Sex was mostly a hidden activity, although some amphorae and twin-handled cups show men fucking in full view of other men, leaving one to wonder just how private a matter sex was, under certain circumstances, in ancient times.

Philemon (See Sources) tells us that the great lawgiver Solon, seeing that young men at times did very unlawful and foolish things due to their inability to find a sexual outlet, allowed prostitutes, male and female, to post themselves throughout Athens in front of their housing, totally naked so as not to fool the client. One paid one's obol and took one's pleasure. A person who sold himself could be used by the client in any way he wished.

Love between men has rarely been a long tranquil river. At times lovers fought, sword in hand, for the love of a boy. Plutarch tells us of Theron who chopped off his own thumb to show his love for his belovèd, and challenged a rival to do the same. Plutarch mentions, too, the case of Konon who killed himself, weary of the tasks imposed on him, and never rewarded, by a youth he wished to have as a belovèd.

Alcibiades had the image of Eros embossed on his shield that Athenaeus states was made of ivory and gold, leaving no doubt as to his amorous pretentions, to the loathing of virtuous Athenians. Having been brought up in the company of the likes of his guardian, Pericles, and Pericles' friends--actors, statesmen, philosophers, as well as the whores Pericles frequented--there was little that the boy didn't know and hadn't experienced from a very scandalized, asked what Anytus was going to do about the theft Anytus answered that, on the contrary, Alcibiades had shown great tenderness in not taking it all. As hope springs eternal in the human breast, Anytus certainly expected that Alcibiades would show other forms of tenderness at another time.

Alcibiades received gifts (or took gifts, as he did at Anytus' dinner) in exchange for love, the penalty for which, at certain times in Athens, was death. Athenian citizens could sell their bodies to whom they wished, but in doing so they could no longer benefit from the rights accorded to citizens. They could no longer speak before the Assembly. They could no longer use the courts for reparation should they in anyway be maligned. If they attempted to do so, they were in real danger of being stoned to death. All that was needed was for someone, anyway, to prove that the person had, at any time in his life, sold himself. A foreigner, on the other hand, someone who was not an Athenian citizen, could prostitute himself/herself without any juridical consequences of any sort. Many foreigners did so and perhaps the totality of male Athenians took advantage of their services at one time or another. When the young Alcibiades left his bedroom at Pericles' home, it was to sleep with a man who had something to offer him, and the ''something'' in question was often money. Alcibiades, as a youth, was a high-class rent-boy who escaped punishment thanks to his guardian, Pericles.

Handsome lads were in great demand in Athens and as the competition to win their favors was fierce, it often cost their aspirants a small fortune, not to speak of the lengthy wooing. Life wasn't always easy for the boys either, as they couldn't show themselves as being too easy for fear of being treated as whores. Stringent laws tried to protect them, but it was clear that when boys wanted to amuse themselves, total surveillance was next to impossible. Foreigners and slaves could be put to death if they tried their hand at boy-love with Athenian citizens. Stringent punishment was reserved for teachers and trainers who had access to them in schools and gymnasiums, access forbidden to older boys over eighteen. Their fathers' male friends were especially carefully watched. If a guardian prostituted the boy he was supposed to protect, he could be stoned. If men couldn't get

Today we have showmen, great orators, warriors and boys who are totally fearless. We have boys who are nearly superhuman in their beauty. There are arrogant boys, willful boys and, naturally, boys who's only interest is in themselves. There are lusty boys who live for sex, taking bodies and offering their own; boys who get off with girls, and boys who go with other boys or other boys and girls. But never have we had a combination of all these as we have in Alcibiades.

He sought ways to remain in the public eye, going so far as to cut off the tail of his dog, its most beautiful attribute. This caused the desired scandal among the Athenians to which he answered, ''Well, I got the attention I was looking for on the one hand, while taking their attention away from the really bad things I've been up to.''

Many men were thought to have slept with him as a boy, as predicted by Philotime in Rocco's *Alcibiades the Schoolboy*. Once, when he disappeared for over a week, Pericles' friends suggested that an alarm should be raised in order to find him. Pericles had been named the boy's guardian since the death of his father when the boy was ten. He now answered that if the lad were dead a general alarm would only find him a little earlier than if there were no alarm at all; if he were alive, on the other hand, the discovery that he had run away would only harm his reputation. Left unsaid was the certainty that if he had run away it was certainly with some man, as no woman could supply him--or would dare supply him--with the luxuries to which he was accustomed. When Alcibiades found out that his guardian, the most respected man in Athens, had defended him, he knew that from then on he could do exactly as he wished. ''For now on,'' he said to his companions, ''the Athenians can kiss my royal ass.''

Anytus, a rich lad, was very found of him and invited Alcibiades to a meal among friends. Alcibiades arrived with companions but proceeded only to the dining room doorway from which he greeted Anytus and his guests, seated before a table with silver and gold tableware. Anytus was, asserts Athenaeus (who goes out of his way to do so), ''Alcibiades' lover''. Alcibiades ordered his companions to gather up half of the tableware, after which he bade Anytus a good evening. When Anytus' friends, into homosexual, heterosexual and bisexual is so accepted that it is difficult to envision a culture, that of Florence, in which a man simply never categorized himself. His quest was pleasure, in whichever direction the quest led him. In this he followed his ancestors the Romans. For them too if a man was horny, he didn't care if the nearest slave at hand was male or female: relief came in the form of a warm orifice. In Ancient Greece, Ancient Rome and Renaissance Florence wives were just one choice among many.

Florentine sex was an inheritance of Greece and Rome in that it concerned men who copulated with boys. Greeks, Romans and Florentines reserved the passive role to boys, the masculine, virile role to men. Being penetrated has never been considered masculine, and today too he-men are tops, not bottoms. Naturally, in alleys, always dark, men did what came naturally, and some boys who became men still preferred ''being taken'', although this was not considered as normal behavior.

Males have always sought each other out in ways incomprehensible to women. They play together, drink together, work together and fight side by side. A soldier thinks nothing of giving his life to save that of a buddy, and even a homo-hating Australian would die for his mate.

THE LIFE OF ALCIBIADES
450 – 404 B.C.
By Michael Hone

The world loves a rogue, and there is no better example than Alcibiades. He was all things to those who crossed his path: intelligent, courageous, ambitious, eloquent in speech, charm personified, so handsome that it's the first adjective employed by biographers and historians alike, sexually versatile, the ideal top to women, the perfect bottom to men; he was totally amoral, as depraved as a teenager, as corrupt as a cop, as streetwise as a delinquent, as pampered as the son of a wallstreeter, as sexy as Paul Newman; he was irreligious, treasonous, and the proof that the gods really do raise to dizzying heights those they wish to utterly destroy.

Sexuality at that time meant omnisexuality. The words homo-hetero-bi wouldn't be invented for another 300 years, and, anyway, if one is to question sexuality it should be to ask why, today, we divide ourselves into one of these three groups, when it's infinitely more varied to open ourselves to absolutely all sexual potentialities, as was the case then. In the words of Molière, *Tout le plaisir de l'amour est dans le changement.*

We learn in Michael Rocke's marvelous *Forbidden Friendships, Homosexuality and Male Culture in Renaissance Italy*, that an official bureau, the Office of the Night, was set up to eliminate sodomy in the Florence of 1432 to 1505, the heart of the Renaissance. Today we use the word sodomy in the sense of male-male sexuality, but we must not forget that back then sodomy was also anything involving both men and women beyond straight cock-cunt sexual intercourse. Cunnilingus was sodomy, as was mutual masturbation. The ultimate penalties were castration and burning at the stake, but because everyone was doing it, nearly everyone got off with a slap on the wrist. Lorenzo *Il Magnifico* de' Medici reigned during this time, the dichotomy being that although the Office of the Night opened its doors, never--thanks to Lorenzo--were Florentines more liberal in the acceptance of male-male sexuality. Boys could do whatever they wanted together, under the title of sexual discovery, fully admitted by parents, never considered *homo*sexuality. Boys bathed naked in the Arno and Tiber rivers, to the immense pleasure of the participants and the men on the banks observing them, just as in ancient Greece the palestra was the ultimate pleasure in a lad's routine (but where adults over age 18 were normally excluded when the athletes were boys).

Lorenzo *Il Magnifico*'s grandfather, Cosimo, had translators translating the Greek humanists, especially Plato, into Italian. He supported the arts, greatly influenced by Greek nudity, and surrounded himself with the great thinkers and writers of the period, one of whom was Antonio Beccadelli who dedicated his *Hermaphroditus* to Cosimo, a work praising love and sex between males.

As Rocke writes, ''sex between males was a common and integral feature of life in'' Florence. Today's divisions of groups risen from the Underworld to claim what was his. Apollo stopped him with a glance, and womanish or not, Hades knew the look in those eyes and trembled, for he was confronted with the god of Light himself, who, next to Hermes, was Zeus' favorite son. So he crept back into the caverns of molten slime that awaited him. Apollo gently picked up the boy and carried him to the Elysian Fields, meadows and islands untouched by sorrow, a blessed land, the home of heroes and the deathless gods, a land free from toil, cradle of perpetual springs and shady groves and bubbling brooks, a cornucopia warmed by its own sun and illumined by its own stars--and eternally cooled by the West Wind, an obligation demanded by Apollo under pain of death.

And there Hyacinth lives, in Elysium, and in us, for the blood he shed nourished the sweet earth, the sweet earth that nourishes us so abundantly to this very day.

Hyacinth

SEX IN THE TIME OF ANTONIO ROCCO: THE RENAISSANCE

As this book deals with homosexuality, I would like to begin by taking an excursion into sexuality during the Renaissance, using Florence as an example.

Cyrus, his precious son was gored by a boar, and his wife, when she learned of her boy's end, took her own life. Now it was the god's turn to suffer.

He and his precious belovèd had spent the morning mountain climbing, they'd swum and exercised, and were now throwing the discus, their bodies, Ovid tells us, were naked and sleek with oil, while their friends, stretched out in the high grass, were chatting as boys do, and applauding the god and the youth. Now, the West Wind had been spying on the couple and had decided that he too would try his hand at boy-love. But when Hyacinth paid him no heed, he became insanely jealous and caused the discus, thrown by Apollo, to fall to the ground where it rebounded and struck the forehead of the sweet youth. Hyacinth fell and where his blood fecundated the earth a bed of hyacinth, rose-red flowers, sprang up. Apollo wailed the loss of his belovèd, arousing Zeus from his noonday sleep. He saw the beauty of the boy entwined in Apollo's arms, as the god of Light shed tears that marked the flowers with spots of white, and like a flower too the boy's head hung lifeless as though cut off at the stem. Thusly were Zeus' eyes opened to the wonder of the love of boys. He immediately took a wise decision: he too would find a companion to while away his days in mutual contentment, his nights in shared bliss, but as a first step, he would make the lad immortal.

He thusly abducted the Trojan youth Ganymede for his bed and--to ward off the smirks--dissimulated the fact by making him his cupbearer.

Soon Man followed suit. The Spartans made boy-love a virile pursuit in which lovers became valorous warriors, preferring death to the betrayal of their loved ones. The Athenians turned boy-love into a philosophical pastime in which, thanks to Eros, the intellectual and the physical were joined to make a new, self-sufficient man. In time the Trojan Aeneas would take the custom to the city he was destined to found on the banks of the Tiber. But this would be neither the virile nor intellectual fusion of body and soul known to the Greeks, but a monstrous, degenerative debauch of painted faces, effeminate bodies and fat slavering perverts.

Apollo had put all his science into reviving Hyacinth's still-warm body but its life had flitted away and already Hades had two of them, but was hugely enlarged into a social event in which Apollo, Hyacinth and their friends were soon all laughing and playing and swimming and exchanging stories and knowledge. And Apollo loved the boys' laughter, so free and uninhibited and carefree and unbridled. While he and Hyacinth gave their youthful bodies in uncomplicated love, around them, hidden in the folds of grass, the other boys did the same, in pairs and in groups. Unrestrained, unruly, totally gratuitous, the end being a liberation of the demanding forces their bodies imposed on them since puberty, and then a race to the river to wash off. Hyacinth never pressured Apollo for something in exchange for the pleasure Apollo accorded him, because their release was mutual and thoroughly fulfilling and totally disinterested. Nor did the boy ever just lie there waiting for something to happen; theirs were two active virilities with never a second of monotony or boredom, something the god had not experienced with a mortal girl.

Apollo

And then Apollo lost what was the most precious being to ever grace his long, long existence. Apollo had been used to inflicting pain, as the time he'd skinned alive the mortal Marsyas when in a musical contest the poor earthling--claiming to be the better musician than Apollo--was outsmarted by the god who could play his lyre rightside-up or upside-down, while Marsyas could only make music through one end of his flute. Apollo and his fellow gods were used to raising those around them to incredible heights, before destroying them utterly, as they did Croesus, making him rich and powerful beyond dreams. Then he lost his empire to than the rest and better built, so unlike Apollo who was a bit hunky around the waist and whose buttocks were a shade large for a man. Hyacinth's were small, round and looked as solid as white marble. Of course, the sun, Apollo's brother Helios, had shaded the boy a tawny brown. The lad had long hair like Apollo, although the lad's fell over his shoulders, while Apollo's was sort of bunched up in a bun over his neck. Hyacinth and Apollo met when Hyacinth went to retrieve a discus he and his friends were throwing back and forth. Hyacinth was surprised to nearly stumble over Apollo, hidden in the high grass, but the god of Light had a nice warm smile and an easy way he'd learned over centuries on Earth, being Immortal and all. They fell into conversation and when his friends went home for dinner Hyacinth preferred to remain and talk with this man whose knowledge was greater than anyone the boy had ever known. Hyacinth soon left because he too was hungry but he returned day after day, his quest for knowledge insatiable. Apollo told stories about kingdoms the boy had never even heard of, and tales about kings and queens and battles and great warriors. They did physical exercises together and soon Apollo was in better shape than at any time in his life.

Lying with boys was normal intimacy for Hyacinth as the girls in Sparta were forced to remain locked up in their parent's homes and boys just naturally fell to giving each other a hand, and other things in preparation for later marriages. Hyacinth was especially attracted to Apollo because the god seemed to combine both sexes. His hips nearly resembled those of women and his breasts were much fuller than a Spartan boy's. In Sparta the lads were all slim-waisted and their pectorals were squared off and as hard as rock. So what happened was more of a surprise to Apollo than to the boy. They had met and now they loved, a new kind of experience for the otherwise very experienced god. In Greek and later Roman love, the man was always the penetrator. That much was clear. But Apollo being Apollo, the swordsman may have been, exceptionally, the young Hyacinth. At any rate, the god of Light was thrilled. Here was someone he could train with, run with, talk with, laugh with, a boy who introduced him to his friends, an intimacy that remained a closed intimacy between the full education, had plenty to eat, and were free to hang around perfume and oil shops, and visit the barber to have their hair cared for and, when older, their nascent beards modishly trimmed.

Apollo would at times leave the stress of giving oracles at Delphi to sprawl out in the meadows of grass and flowers next to the Spartan river Eurotas. At the time Delphi was the most important site in Greece, just after Mount Olympus itself. Delphi. In the beginning the gods freed two high-flying eagles, one from the East, the other from the West. They met on the lofty crags of a great mountain that loomed over a jagged valley and the far-off port of Cirrha. Here was the sacred center of the universe; here was the spiritual navel of the Hellenes; here was Delphi, home of Apollo.

For Apollo had left his birthplace on Cycladic Delos to teach Man wisdom by revealing to him the future. Apollo traveled to the heights of Mount Parnassus where he destroyed the snake-like dragon, Python, its guardian. Then, with the help of the Muses and the consent of Mother Earth, he recruited sailors from a passing Cretan ship whom he made priests, and irreproachable villagers from the nearby village of Krissa whom he ordained priestesses, sometimes called Pythonesses in memory of the dragon. He built a temple, initiated the love of the arts, taught moderation and humaneness in all things, and himself tried to exemplify the virtuous life.

But as any lad knows, at times a boy needs more than moderation and virtue. At times he wants to let out all the stops. That's why Apollo chose the meadows around Eurotas. He loved clear streams and to bask in the sun and watch the Spartan boys, naked as the day, come down to swim and horse around. It made Apollo smile to see lads as frisky as yearlings, without a care in the world, while he had to continually divvy up oracles about which king was legitimate and which was not, which state would win a war if it crossed a certain river; and what the future held in store for this lass and her beau, or for that king and his kingdom, not to mention his obligation to adjudicate over poisonings, incests, murders and crucifixions.

The boy the others called Hyacinth was clearly better looking

Antonio Rocco

Incredibly, Rocco was a priest, as well as a writer and Aristotelian philosophy teacher. He wrote *Alcibiades the School Boy* in 1630. It's first publication, in 1652, was destroyed due to the filth of its content, all but a few surviving copies, and was republished in 1862. It was again found filthy and again largely destroyed. Philotime is modeled after Socrates and the text is considered the world's first homoerotic novel.

Antonio Rocco tells us that Alcibiades began his schooling under the ''venerable'' teacher Philotime. The boy was of the age of Ganymede when Zeus immortalized him, thanks to his son Apollo. This is their story: Apollo claimed that it was the beauty of Hyacinth that lured him into night games at the side of lads. Now, Hyacinth was a Spartan, born during the Mycenaean period, long before the laws of Lycurgus came into effect, making life in Sparta more difficult. After Lycurgus, boys were raised in the women's quarters until age seven, after which they were put in barracks and formed groups called herds ruled over by an older boy known as the boy-herder, who wielded a whip. They slept on reed beds, wore red cloaks, ate a sickening broth and were taught to forage for food because there was never enough in their communal messes. From age twelve the boys were free to choose older friends with whom they formed a sexual bond, friends who taught them what they needed to know about warfare and loyalty to the Spartan state. But when Hyacinth was born--before the laws of Lycurgus--Sparta was a city much like all the others in Greece, much like Athens, where boys Hyacinth's age could get a know for certain that when Alcibiades left the banquet he took a good breath of fresh air, and went straight to find a warm bed with a warm boy to fill it.

At any rate Alcibiades knew the truth of Theognis' words:

I play, enjoying my youth. For I shall lie
A long time under the earth, when life is gone.
Deaf as a stone I'll leave forever the sun's warmth;
Fine though I was, I shall see nothing more.

Whether in truth Socrates did manage to rein in his libido will never be known, but on this very scene from Plato's *Banquet* Cicero muses that it was nonetheless curious that men like Socrates were always willing to give a helping hand to beautiful boys like Alcibiades, but never ever to ugly ones.

ANTONIO ROCCO
1586 – 1653

The book *Alcibiades the Schoolboy* was originally written in Italian, in 1630, and then translated into French by, *perhaps*, Édouard Cléder. Due to the expense of the English version--when found--I decided to translate it myself from the French, my second language, into English, my first. I've at times inserted the French translation so that Francophiles can follow the text in the original. The reader will remark that Alcibiades, a child, uses, most often, adult expressions and adult reasoning. The penalty for a teacher touching a student, as Philotime touches Alcibiades, was death. Alcibiades reminded his master of this on several occasions. Indeed, Philotime was playing a very serious game (2). During the time of Antonio Rocco, the Renaissance, the death penalty was reserved for those who forced boys. Otherwise men were fined and given a slap on the wrist, although burning at the stake was nonetheless applied in several cases (3). In the text the boy's anus is referred to as his flower or garden, his cock is, at times, his bird, a fig is a cunt, and sperm is dew.

make of me a better person?'' Socrates agreed that it was indeed his aim to make him better, and so saying, he closed his eyes and man and boy spent the night ... platonically. The next morning Alcibiades recounted that it was as if he had slept with his father or brother, and then went on to add, with all the modesty of those who are beautiful, that he was forced to admire the inner strength of Socrates, because he had resisted the body of the lad a full night! Xenophon confirmed that Alcibiades needed Socrates because of the philosopher's immense ''competence in discourses and in strategic action.'' He added that Alcibiades might have known about Socrates' total control over his pulsations and was thusly certain to be able to offer himself without the slightest risk of being abused.

As the banquet proceeded, Socrates and Plato felt they had to absolve man and boy relationships by finding a virtuous justification for them. This was apparently easy in man-to-woman attachments because the man and the woman worked in a virtuous tandem, in that he gave his sperm and she became physically pregnant with a child, this being the first virtue; the second virtue resided in the fact that, thanks to his progeny, a man became immortal. Man and boy relations could be virtuous when the players passed on to each other knowledge and wisdom, especially when the lover did so to his belovèd. The belovèd became pregnant in terms of his soul, and his child was the virtue his lover had implanted in him (knowledge/wisdom). Socrates claimed that without this kind of insemination the sex act was useless. Because Alcibiades was incapable of giving virtue, said Socrates, he was doomed to mortality. For Alcibiades things were far simpler: the eroticism of his inseminating a handsome youth was perfect fulfillment in itself. We don't know if these two philosophers succeeded in making the boy feel guilty, we don't know if they were even sincere in disseminating such nonsense. We do know that Alcibiades tried to seduce Socrates despite his age and ugliness, perhaps to show the philosopher that the philosopher really did care for the physical aspect of love, just like everyone else. (If Alcibiades were as handsome as the ancients say--and only half as wonderful as he thought himself to be--then the temptation must have been truly difficult for Socrates.) But we

THE LIFE OF ALCIBIADES
450 – 404 B.C.
page 13

SEX IN THE TIME OF ALCIBIADES: ANCIENT GREECE
As seen through the Trial of Aeschines against Timarchus
page 28

ALCIBIDES THE SCHOOLBOY
By Antonio Rocco
Translated from the French by Michael Hone
page 31

SOURCES
page 61

INTRODUCTION

Plato offers us, in his *Banquet,* an incredibly revealing side of Alcibiades, the most beautiful, the most sought-after Athenian of his day. Alcibiades knew that Socrates could give him everything he needed to complete his rise to political power: knowledge, argumentation, rhetoric, dialectic, strategizing and worldliness. As for Alcibiades, he had only his physical perfection to offer in return. He thusly invited the philosopher to a dinner in which he deployed his every charm. His surprise was great when his guest, finding that Alcibiades had dismissed all his servants, did not immediately make clear, in one of the multiply forms that men employ to assuage their lust, his interest in the boy. In fact, after eating, Socrates rose to leave. Telling Socrates that the hour was late, Alcibiades suggested he remain the night. When he did so, Alcibiades crept into bed, beside him, and told Socrates that he knew of no man as deserving as he to gain access to his beauty, and it would be stupid if they didn't seek pleasure one with the other. ''After all,'' continued the boy, ''who better than you can

My books include: *Cellini, Caravaggio, Cesare Borgia, Renaissance Murders, Greek Homosexuality, ARGO, Buckingham, RENT BOYS, Homoerotic Art (in full color), Sailors and Homosexuality, The Essence of Being Gay, John (Jack) Nicholson, THE SACRED BAND, German Homosexuality, Gay Genius, SPARTA, Charles XII of Sweden, Mediterranean Homosexual Pleasure, CAPRI, Boarding School Homosexuality, HUSTLERS, American Homosexual Giants, TROY, Christ has his John, I have my George: The History of British Homosexuality, Homosexual Pornography* and my autobiography: *Michael Hone: His World, His Loves.*

I live in the South of France.

CONTENTS

INTRODUCTION
page 3

ANTONIO ROCCO
1586 – 1653
page 5

SEX IN THE TIME OF ANTONIO ROCCO: THE RENAISSANCE
page 11

ALCIBIADES THE SCHOOLBOY

By Antonio Rocco

Introduced and translated by
Michael Hone

Revised Edition © 2018